"Tyler Edwards draws a powerful and poignant parallel in *Zombie Church* that will resonate culturally with readers. This book is captivating with its vibrant and at times scary renditions of the similarities between what Edwards calls the 'undead' and what is supposed to be the body of Christ. Thankfully, there is a cure for the Zombie church! This is a powerful read, full of hope and challenge for the church to come to life, rise up out of its pews, and be the glorious bride of Christ we are called to be. *Zombie Church* is 'dead on.'"

—STEPHANIE FREED, Executive Director,
Rapha House

"I have never watched a zombie movie, but I have seen a few churches that 'have a reputation of being alive, but . . . are dead' (Rev. 3:1). So has Tyler Edwards. In this book, with cultural wit and biblical wisdom, he calls us to be the living, vibrant body of Christ. Someone once said, Learn from others' mistakes because you won't have time to make them all yourself. Tyler candidly shares his own mistakes and lets us watch his growth as a leader. With so many recent books bashing the church, you'll be encouraged to hear this young pastor's love for the bride of Christ, and you'll be challenged to lead your church into the abundant life found in Jesus."

—MATT PROCTOR, President,
Ozark Christian College

"For all of us who have ever attended First Church of the Frigidaire, Edwards' book will be warmly welcomed. It is a fair-minded and tenderhearted critique of the church from a practicing pastor. His appraisal, however, comes with a twist. He uses those B-rate zombie films that fill late-night cable channels as a metaphor for the church. Since I'm not a zombie movie fan, the idea seemed kitschy at first. With each passing chapter, however, my mantra was: "Well, yeah, that's right!" This novel lens of zombies allows the reader to see afresh the desperate need for awaking in the church."

—MARK MOORE, PhD, Professor of New Testament,
Ozark Christian College

ZOMBIE CHURCH

BREATHING LIFE BACK INTO THE BODY OF CHRIST

TYLER EDWARDS

Published by Kregel Publications, a division of Kregel, Inc., P.O. Box 2607, Grand Rapids, MI 49501.

Italics in Scripture quotations indicate emphasis added by the author.

Library of Congress Cataloging-in-Publication Data
Edwards, Tyler, 1984–
Zombie church : breathing life back into the body of Christ / Tyler Edwards.
p. cm.
Includes bibliographical references (p. 213).
1. Church renewal. I. Title.
BV600.3.E395 2011 262.001'7—dc23 2011017867

ISBN 978-0-8254-2459-5

Printed in the United States of America

11 12 13 14 15 / 5 4 3 2 1

For my wonderful wife, Erica:
You are a constant blessing and encouragement.
You are an inspiration and a wonderful example of what the life of a Christ follower looks like.

For my mother, who gave me life, and passion to write, and brought me to a relationship with Christ.

For the glory of my Lord Jesus Christ: my hope is that this book will be pleasing in Your sight.

You diligently study the Scriptures because you think that by them you possess eternal life. These are the Scriptures that testify about me, yet you refuse to come to me to have life.

John 5:39–40

CONTENTS

ACKNOWLEDGMENTS

I want to acknowledge, with great gratitude, several people who have played a significant role in my life.

First, my wonderful wife, Erica: You give me strength and encouragement and help refine me into a better man. Thank you, dear, for everything you do and for your constant willingness to put up with me.

I would also like to especially thank my mother, Vicki: You raised me on a steady diet of Jesus, and I would not be the man I am without you. Thank you, too, for all the time you put into helping me edit and revise this book.

I would like to thank one of my professors, Mark Moore, whose teachings and dedication to the study of the life of Jesus inspired me and showed me the true meaning of loving God with all one's mind.

I also want to express my gratitude to a few people who helped me get the vision for *Zombie Church* moving in the right direction: Eric Dwyer, Trent McClure, and Kirra Antrobus. Your insights and ideas helped make this book so much more than it would have been without you. And Miranda Gardner, who found my book and was willing to give a first-time writer a chance.

Finally, I want to thank everyone at Cornerstone and the people I have been blessed to do ministry with. You do not know what you mean to me and the important roles you have played in my life. Thank you all.

INTRODUCTION

There are Zombie churches among us. The undead church. Where undead persons feast. Where genuine life has been lost, and in its place is something . . . scary. Lifeless.

In some churches, the loss of life is obvious; in others it is more subtle. Have you ever walked into a church where everything appeared normal? Everyone was smiling and seemed so happy because, after all, smiling at church is what Christians are supposed to do. Everyone was personable, but no one was really personal. It might even have seemed like everyone's friendliness kept you at arm's length. How many people greeted you at church but never really took the time to get to know you? Have you ever gone to a church service where nothing seemed wrong per se but you just felt like *something* was missing?

Some of us have not only wandered into these churches, but we have sung in their worship, listened to their sermons, and returned week after week. Some of us have become part of these churches. Some of us have lived our whole lives in a Zombie church.

Of course, we can only endure this for so long. In recent years there has been a steady movement away from organized religion. Christian writers are becoming more critical of the church and less hopeful about its survival in the future. Some have even gone so far as to say that the organized church must be done away with.[1] In *Revolution*, George Barna writes: "If the local church is the hope of the world, then the world has no hope."[2]

When Christian leaders are telling people to abandon the church like a sinking ship or implying as much, then the problem has reached a whole new level. It's easy to look at the church and all of its flaws and to become jaded; when the church gets things wrong, it's easy to forget about what the church gets right. The church was instituted by God and He has a plan for her. Certainly, the church isn't perfect, but there's still hope for her.

I'm sure most of us have heard someone say, "I can't stand the church because it's full of liars and hypocrites." This is, of course, a direct result of the fact that the people who go to church *are* liars, hypocrites, and fakes. Mahatma Gandhi nailed the problem: "I like your Christ, I do not like your Christians. Your Christians are so unlike your Christ." Honestly, there is no better way to identify the problem than that. Christians are not enough like Christ.

"The greatest single cause of atheism in the world today is Christians who acknowledge Jesus with their lips then walk out the door and deny Him by their lifestyle."[3] The world does not understand verbal devotion without appropriate action. Those who say one thing and do another are labeled as "hypocrites." If we honestly look at how those in the church act sometimes, the accusation seems fair. We claim to be followers of Jesus imitating His life, but that is exactly the problem. What we have is imitation life. So many Christians do not live their lives with Jesus at the center. Our words and our deeds are not projecting the same message, and so people walk away from both. The church is infected. This is the condition we need to cure. My purpose in writing this is not to complain; there are plenty of

The church is not a decaying corpse, but she is sick with a disease.

resources available if that is what you are seeking. My goal is to address a problem, reveal its significance, and illuminate the path to healing this condition that faces the contemporary church.

As we look at the problems facing the church, the easiest solution does seem to be to walk away. But simply walking away from the church because she is broken is not what God would have us do. The church is Christ's bride, and we are Christ's followers; shouldn't we then fight for the bride of our Lord?

The church is not a decaying corpse, but she is sick with a disease. There is an antidote, however, and rather than deserting the church, we ought to find a way to cure the disease running through her body.

Why Talk About Zombies?

I confess: I have a taste for cheesy horror films. These are movies that lack the skill or budget to actually be scary, and despite their great efforts end up as more of a comedy with monsters than anything else. Bad acting, bad dialogue, typically a bad story, and bad costume design can make for a good laugh. My favorites of these films are zombie movies.

Most zombie movies try to offer a unique explanation for where the zombies originate. The explanation is rarely, if ever, satisfying, but *something* happens and all of a sudden people start turning into zombies, and *somehow* the infection spreads. The one common thread with zombie movies is the nature of the zombies themselves. Neither dead nor alive, they are beings trapped in a mindless existence.

Zombies do not produce anything. They do not accomplish anything. All they do is wander around aimlessly, consuming everything in their path (including non-zombies). They are a corrupt and destructive force that taints all they come in contact with. Zombies act like they are alive, but they are dead. They just don't know it yet.

Yes, there are zombies in our churches. Not only that, but this seems to be a growing trend. The doors are open, the people show up faithfully, the songs are sung. But that's it. So many American churches today are filled with people whose spiritual lives consist of little more than showing up to church on Sunday morning and, for the superspiritual, maybe once in the middle of the week. We have become experts at going through the motions, but these motions are all we go through. I can't help but wonder if God didn't have something more in mind for His church. It seems that something is missing.

In looking at the church in North America today and comparing it to the church in Acts 2 and 4, I can't help but think that we have lost the basic foundation of what it means to be the church.[4] I have heard horror stories (no pun intended) of churches splitting because two families couldn't get along or factions didn't agree on a method of evangelism. Shouldn't we have more important things to worry about? When our mission as the body of Christ can be overshadowed by something like building decorations, we have gotten onto the wrong path.

It seems we make Jesus the Lord of Sunday morning, then kick Him off the throne as we leave the church building. It's sort of like having a one-night stand with Jesus every week. We sing songs like "I Surrender All," when we really mean "I surrender some."

Objective

I have gone to church my whole life. I have sat in the seats. I have done the song and dance. I have prayed, read the Scriptures, given communion meditations, served communion, shown up for special events, participated in the greeting time, and both listened to and preached hundreds of sermons. Jesus has been a part of my life since I was a child. I have done just about everything there is to do inside the church walls. I know how to go through the motions as well as anyone. But I'm tired of that. I'm bored. I'm bored coming to the same services every week singing songs, preaching sermons, and going home. I want something more out of church, and I suspect most of you do too.

Boredom comes from a lack of purpose. When someone without Christ gets bored, it makes sense; they are living life with no purpose. But what about the bored Christian? I think the reason we get bored in the church is not because we do not have a purpose but because we have forgotten our purpose. When a church exists without purpose, it slowly turns into a Zombie church.

In this book, we will look at the church in terms of what it is, what it ideally should be, and how to traverse the gap. People are starting to realize that there is something wrong with the church. We may not all recognize what the problem is, but clearly we are starting to feel that there is one. My goal is to identify what is missing and to look at possible ways to fix it so that the church can become what it was created by God to be. The church is the bride of Christ, and that alone makes her worth fighting for.

Zombie churches might not look any different from healthy churches, but they are missing an essential ingredient: life.

This book should be a reminder of the purpose and function of the church so we may be better able to identify the healthy churches from the dying ones. Zombie churches might not look any different from healthy churches, but they are missing an essential ingredient: life. Before we can fix the problem, however, we must identify it. If there is a disease that creates Zombie churches, my hope is that this book will help lead us to the cure.

The church is the bride of Christ, the fellowship of God's children. It is not an archaic or optional assembly. In other words, it is not something to give up on, no matter how much it resembles the living dead. Doctors do not just give up on sick patients because they are unhealthy; good doctors search for the problem, the root cause, and try to cure it. God is gracious and is willing to breathe life back into stagnant structures if we will truly seek His presence. This book isn't an epitaph but an elixir. The condition that besets the church is certainly life threatening, but the church isn't dead yet.

Chapter One

Warning Signs

Imagine getting ready to attend a new church for the first time on a Sunday morning. You wake up early, the sun is shining, the birds are chirping. You get dressed in your best outfit and head downstairs. You breathe deeply of fresh morning air. Your wonderful children are awake and smiling, not a hair out of place. You sit down to a delicious breakfast together. You tell your children how much fun they are going to have learning about Jesus and making new friends.

Since you have just moved to this new community, you yourself have been waiting all week for this opportunity to build friendships. You find yourself filled with a nervous excitement as you start the car. On the way to the church your heart starts to race as you imagine the awesome people you are going to meet. You pull into the parking lot. You hold hands with your youngest as you walk up to the beautiful double glass doors. You smile at the greeter. He silently places a bulletin in your hands.

You expected to find life in an engaging community, but rather than a warm greeting you are met with blank expressions of complete indifference. People flow by as if you are invisible, or perhaps a nuisance. You try to figure out where you are supposed to go but no one stops to help you. The halls clear and there you are, awkwardly trying to find your place. You reach the sanctuary and enter. Acutely aware of the whispering going on all around, you make your way to a seat. As you sit you think, *Here we go, now that we're settled in someone will greet us.*

The music begins to play and everyone around you starts to sing. They sing songs about joy, but it appears that they forgot to tell their faces. The minister gets up to speak; he prays and then begins. His message turns into one big, long complaint. He drags on for what seems like days, criticizing how everyone lives their lives and whining about the choices other people make that he doesn't agree with. At the end of it all, you feel tired and beat up.

The service ends and everyone stands up and shuffles out. You leave feeling like an ex who showed up for a family reunion, and you start to wonder if maybe there is something wrong with you. When you left the house you felt invigorated and excited with the possibilities. When you return you feel like someone has sucked the life out of you. Have you ever been there?

So many churches in America today have lost sight of their purpose. It is this loss of purpose that turns our churches into Zombie churches. People come expecting to find life and what they get is . . . something else. It's bad enough walking into a room and being attacked by a horde of brain-hungry zombies, but on a *Sunday morning, in church*—that is the worst! It is also probably the last thing you'd expect. We don't expect to be welcomed at the post office, but we expect civility. We don't expect a warm embrace at McDonald's, but we do expect service. When we go to a church and leave without experiencing Christian fellowship, there is a problem. Even those who are not ardent churchgoers can sense that something is missing.

I know most of us have never had a real-life zombie encounter. This is likely because zombies are not real. At least most educated people in Haiti would probably agree, though belief in zombies among the rest of Haitians is apparently universal. This isn't surprising since zombies appear in the stories and folklore of Haiti and are a legendary phenomenon in voodoo cult. Researchers studying Haitian culture have even analyzed "zombie powder" in an attempt to explain a particular incident of zombiism some thirty years ago.[1] In any case, it might seem strange to use creatures that (probably) do not actually exist as a metaphor for the church, but the similarities are striking.

I'm going to assume that you are not a zombie expert. So what is a zombie? A zombie is defined (yes, by the dictionary) as "the body of a dead person given the semblance of life."[2] Zombies are dead bodies faking life.

When we look at the characteristics of zombies, you might start seeing them in the church . . . maybe even in the mirror. Zombies are creatures that, at least at a distance, appear to be living human beings. At closer proximity, it is apparent that they are "undead" (behaving as if they are alive even though they are not). Not really living, not really dead. This is the point that connects with the church. When I use "dead" in reference to the church, I don't so much mean hellbound and hopeless (though that may occasionally be true) but having lost a connection to life. Zombies only imitate life. Their actions and the externals are right, but there is something missing from the inside. Left untreated, zombiism is fatal to the church.

Zombies are dead bodies faking life.

Living churches exist. You can walk in the doors of a living church and feel overwhelmed with the presence of the Spirit of God. But not all churches are alive. Life is found in what a church does with Jesus and how they go about following Him in their community. When the church neglects the commission of Jesus—stops ministering to the poor and the hurting and stops sharing the love of God with others—then it stops living. It just exists and keeps on existing. Undead. How can a church offer the eternal life of God if it does not have life in its midst?

So what makes a church body living or dead? The same thing that makes a human body living or dead: whether or not there is a spirit residing in it. Zombies still have a body—they often still look the same—but they are disconnected from the spirit. *The* Spirit. The Holy Spirit is like a six-year-old

Jesus calls us to a journey that leads to eternity.

after a candy frenzy. He doesn't sit still for very long. He is an innovator: prompting movement, triggering change, instigating adaptation, mixing things up. And we need to keep up. The Holy Spirit is always culturally relevant. When He speaks, He speaks in a way the people understand. He is the same, but He is willing to alter the venue and style of His communication to fit with the people He is communicating to.

Jesus does not call us to a localized destination where knowing and believing all the right things grants you access to eternity regardless of how you live. Jesus calls us to a journey that leads to eternity. It's not a destination; it's a lifelong adventure.

Food is also necessary for human life—both physical and spiritual. You've heard the saying, "You are what you eat!" Life or death is a result of what we feed on. Living Christians feed on the life that Jesus offers while zombies feed on rules and rituals. If you are feeding on Jesus, then naturally you are becoming more like Him. If you are feeding on traditions or laws or denominational differences, then what you are eating doesn't sustain life.

Dead Churches Faking Life

The church is supposed to offer the source of eternal life, Jesus. Some do exactly that. Sadly, others do not. Even in places where the lawn is mowed, the music plays, and meetings are scheduled, life can be absent. Just because things are moving does not mean there is true life. Some churches have hollow motions. Healing is not administered, joy is not experienced, minds are not edified, and people are not changed. One of the best tests to see if a church is truly alive is to ask the question, if the church closed its doors would anyone outside of it even notice?

A Zombie church is any church that has lost its focus on God. The Spirit of God is what gives life to a church. It is not a matter of going through the right motions that conjures life in the Spirit. Our efforts to control the Holy Spirit are like a man standing in the middle of a river trying to control its flow by sticking his hands in the water. The Holy Spirit is not a resource to be tapped or harnessed but a power source to remain connected to. The life He offers comes from giving control over to Him. (Yes, the Holy Spirit is a "He" rather than "it"; He is just as personal and as much God as the Father and the Son.) Instead of trying to control the river with feeble hands, the man should fall back into it and allow the powerful currents to carry him. Believers need to move *with* the Spirit.

When the church fails to adapt to the movement of the Spirit, it can easily lose its connection to life. When this happens some churches realize it and pursue the Spirit, desperate to catch up, to regain that connection to life. Others respond by establishing a great list of rules and practices in hopes that if they go back to doing things the way they were done when the Spirit was there, then life will return; then the Holy Spirit will come back to them.

The Spirit of God is not something we control. The living Spirit does not answer to us and is not a mechanized device to be programmed. The Spirit is a powerful force of transformation that moves in our lives and in the church. As He moves we are forced to choose between following or standing still. Churches that do the latter have a tendency of turning into the reanimated dead.[3]

Let me tell you about Mary. Mary was a very kind woman, thoughtful and considerate of others. She had grown up in the church and was developing her relationship with God. When she was around thirty, she moved with her husband to a new town in the "Bible Belt"—that part of the country where churches adorn every street corner. In talking with her one day, I learned that she would not go to church anymore. I asked her why. She proceeded to tell me that when she first moved to the area she was looking for a church to attend with her family. She walked into a church in town and she was wearing a skirt that went down a good bit past her knees and a plain T-shirt that was not tight or low-cut or anything. (Mary paused for a moment, a little choked up, then continued.) When she walked in, there was a crowd of people in the foyer. She hardly made it through the door when the pastor of the church walked up to her and said, "If you are going to dress like a whore, get out of my church!" That was it. So she left, and she never went back.

I was appalled. It's bad enough when people in the church, who may be there for the wrong reasons, say something rude, but the *pastor*? A pastor should know better! Where many Christians and even church leaders today differ from Jesus is clear: Jesus offers love when He has every right to judge, while we offer judgment when we have little grounds for it.

When a church stops behaving like Jesus, it stops offering the life it advertises.

In John 8 the religious leaders bring a woman who was caught in adultery before Jesus and ask Him what to do with her. They dragged this woman out of the house and likely did not take the time to clothe her. It is probable that this woman was cast at Jesus' feet naked, having been caught in sexual sin. Jesus' response is not, "Look at how you are dressed, you whore; get out of My presence." Jesus defends the woman. He offers her grace and tells her to go and sin no more. The point that I want to make is, when a church stops behaving like Jesus, it stops offering the life it advertises.

Hypocrisy

I knew a girl who came to church every Sunday and acted like a saint, but when Friday night came around, she was drunk at a party or having sex with her boyfriend. She exuded passion about following Jesus, but it never left the church building. She had no apparent remorse. She even felt it was OK for her to rebuke someone who was dancing too much at church. Do you see the contradiction? She attacked someone who was acting in a way she felt was inappropriate while she herself engaged in what was clearly sinful behavior. She was that girl with a plank in her eye trying to take a speck out of someone else's (Matt. 7:3).

This defines hypocrisy. She played the good-Christian card at church and then did her own thing the rest of the time. What makes this worse, however, is how we hear her story. The people who see hypocrisy in others are usually trying to ignore it in themselves. It is easy to condemn this girl for her hypocrisy, but in so doing, we also condemn ourselves. When we judge her, aren't we doing the same thing she did? I have often found myself with a great plank in my eye and a smile on my face because I saw so many specks in the eyes of others. We often criticize others for their faults while we ourselves have personal sins we have been unable to conquer. Of course, we must not condone sinful behavior, but we must remember that we ourselves are sinners, or we become modern-day Pharisees.

I have often found myself with a great plank in my eye and a smile on my face.

What scares me is that when I hear stories like this, I am almost encouraged. I am glad other people sin and act like hypocrites, because it makes me feel better about myself. That's a problem. Jesus would never rejoice in the sin of others. When Jesus corrected people's sins, He did so with patience and with love, which I notice is rarely the way I deal with them. When we stop following Jesus' example; we stop following Jesus. Rebuke without love is merely accusation, and God is not the accuser. When we rebuke others without love in our hearts, we are acting like Satan. I guess the thing that really scares me is that when I look at how the church often deals with sin, it doesn't resemble the way Jesus dealt with sin.

The church has a virus. That virus is running rampant through many of those who are a part of it. As the church begins to move further from Jesus in its behavior and treatment of others, it slowly pulls away from its source of life. This can only go on for so long before the infection takes over and the church becomes a Zombie church.

Stagnancy

In a little town not too far from where I went to college was a church that had about thirty or forty people in regular attendance. They brought in a very passionate, young preacher. After he'd been there for about eight months, laying the groundwork and building relationships with the people, he started pushing for them to do something.

He wanted to see the church reach out to the community and to grow. The church leaders balked; they didn't like that the preacher was trying to grow the church. They fired him. No reason was given other than that they liked things the way they were and they didn't want someone changing them. They wanted a biblical message with the call to action surgically removed. Have you ever walked into a church like that? It is almost as if everyone glares at you for "intruding" into their perfect setting. There may have been life there once, but now it is gone.

If you can't imagine a church like this, let me help you. While in Bible college, I went to a church in Arkansas where my friend Eric was preaching. This church had nine members. It did not have nine members because it was a vibrant group of believers launching into a new region, hoping to set their town on fire with the love of God. No. It had once housed sleeping infants, restless toddlers and children, adults of every size and shape. It had once been a church with life and love and energy—until . . . The facts of the "until" I do not know. Perhaps the town's economy changed and people moved away. Perhaps the church itself changed, split, or atrophied. For whatever reason, the church had not prospered.

At the time of my visit, not one of the Nine Survivors was under the age of fifty-five. Several of them had been born and raised in this very church. And they intended to die there.

Every week between Sunday school and the worship service, they pulled on a rope that ran from the bell tower down into the foyer. This bell rang for an entire minute before service every week. Each gong was a loud invitation to all, but the gongs just echoed in empty streets. The piano was badly out of tune, the hymnals cracked and missing pages. They hired a Sunday-only preacher to bring a sermon and give an invitation. After a month of this, Eric asked them if he could come down on a Saturday and have a fellowship picnic with them at a park. They said no.

After a few weeks, Eric noticed that the baptismal was covered with a sheet of plywood that had been painted blue. "Why is the baptismal covered?" he asked.

The lady who played the piano answered, "A little boy fell in it awhile back and got hurt."

"Oh, I see. You didn't want anyone to drown," Eric said, assuming he understood.

Then, as if there was nothing wrong with the words she was about to say, the lady responded, "Oh, there hasn't been any water in this baptismal for years!"

After his first few months, Eric asked them if it would be OK if he didn't do the invitation every week—because, well, no one new showed up.

The man who was basically in charge of the church told Eric, "I don't know that I am comfortable coming to church without an invitation." Eric wanted to ask, "An invitation to what? Everyone in this church has been a Christian for two or three times the length of my life."

One week, before the bell ringing, a young woman showed up. The room was divided into two rows of pews facing a big iron-clad pulpit at center stage. All of the regulars sat on the far end of the left side of the church. This new lady came in and sat down on the right. No one said hello. No one walked over to introduce themselves. During the greeting time, the nine faithful members all warmly embraced each other without so much as a smile or nod to their guest. In fact, throughout the service the members stared at her like she was a monster.

This lady could have been walking into a church for the first time in her life. When people go to a new church, they are usually looking for something. What if this woman had shown up that day because she was looking for Jesus? The best impression of Jesus she received is that Jesus is cold, impersonal, and only cares about His own. And that's because, as you know, people see Jesus by looking at those who follow Him. So when the church fails to show the love and hospitality of Jesus, how can the world see it? Jesus tells us to go to the world, and yet sometimes God is gracious enough to bring the world to us. We cannot afford to miss opportunities like that.

This church was missing something. The doors were open; the services were held. But this church was dead. The Nine Survivors went to church because it is what they had done their entire lives. For them, church wasn't about a relationship with Christ. Church was what you do on Sunday morning. We could learn from their faithfulness and dedication in staying with a church for so long, but this church was missing something no church should ever go without. This was the first time I realized I was in a Zombie church.

Living Among the Dead

On the Sunday morning following Jesus' crucifixion, Mary and a few other women went to Jesus' tomb with spices they had prepared. This was a common burial practice that prevented the dead from . . . smelling like the dead. When they arrived at the tomb, they found that the stone had been rolled away. They looked inside, but Jesus' body was nowhere to be found. While they were there two angels appeared.

> In their fright the women bowed down with their faces to the ground, but the men said to them, "Why do you look for the living among the dead? He is not here; he has risen! Remember how he told you, while he was still with you in Galilee: 'The Son of Man must be delivered into the hands of sinful men, be crucified and on the third day be raised again.'" (Luke 24:5–7)

The angels ask: "Why do you look for the living among the dead?" Sometimes our answer is: "Because that's what you do on Sunday morning." We seek life where life does not exist. Some churches look for Jesus in all the wrong places. They seek Him in the rules: don't do this, don't go there, don't do that. They expect to find Him in the laws and traditions. They search for Him in routines and theological debates. They seek the living among the dead. They look to religion to offer the life that only comes from a relationship with Jesus Christ.

Life will not be found in a denomination, in a practice, in a custom, in a rule, or in a building.

When you look in the wrong places, you will not find what you seek. If the church is going to share in the resurrected life of Jesus, then it must start seeking Jesus and just Jesus. The church needs to stop trying to get the most answers right. Life will not be found in a denomination, in a practice, in a custom, in a rule, or in a building. Life is not granted to those who get the most answers right in this world. Life comes from the grace of God to all who will accept it. It is time for the church to stop looking for life in the wrong places and to start focusing everything they have on Jesus, for He is truly life.

Restoring Life to the Undead Church

What is a Zombie church? A Zombie church is a church that goes through the motions. It may behave like a healthy, living church, but the Zombie church has lost its connection to life. The people have the name of Jesus. They sing praise to Him. But it has been a long time since they really lived their lives for Him. Zombie churches may do the right things, but they do them for the wrong reasons. Our "heart" is reflected not just in what we do but by the motivation and determination with which we do it. It is possible for us to look good by following all the proper religious protocol while holding on to wickedness and sin. It is even possible for us to do good things for bad reasons. As the saying goes, intent always precedes content.

Imagine two men making a toy: one of them is doing it to get paid; the other is making a gift for his daughter. While they may be carrying out the same task, there will be a distinct difference in the investment they make on this object. The man who is making this toy so he can get what he wants (his paycheck) will do it as well as required to earn his reward. The man making the toy for his daughter on the other hand will strive to make the toy to the best of his ability.

Why the difference? The first man's motivation is practical. What he's doing is simply a means to an end. He can do the right thing and make a nice toy, but he will do it only insomuch as he sees the benefit in doing it. The second man is not motivated by self-preservation but by love. Thus, while the product may look the same, the heart behind it is not.

In reading the Gospels, I've noticed how frustrating the Pharisees and

Sadducees are to Jesus. In John 4 we see Jesus interacting with the Samaritan woman, a woman who has lived a sinful life. Jesus treats her with kindness and love despite the fact that she doesn't seem to get who He is. Yet when He encounters the religious leaders who use their "connection to God" for personal gain and come to Jesus in efforts to trap Him, Jesus often rebukes them. Unlike man, Jesus looks to the condition of the heart. To those who come honestly seeking Him, Jesus is gentle and patient, even when they make mistakes. Peter's life is an example of just how much patience Jesus has with those who honestly seek Him. Yet in Luke 11 we see Him criticizing the religious leaders again and again. Jesus knew their motives. While the disciples wanted to learn, the religious leaders wanted to trap Him. In the church, we are not just supposed to do the right things; we need to do the right things for the right reasons.

One of the beautiful things about Jesus is that He doesn't demand perfection. We may get things wrong in our efforts to follow Him. We may hurt people who come looking for Jesus without ever knowing it. In His grace, God doesn't hold our sins against us. Jesus doesn't ask us to get it all right. He just asks us to honestly come to Him. We will never be perfect, but we can always look more like Jesus. It needs to be said: God is cool. No matter how many times we get it wrong, He is still right there to offer us life. Who else does that? Who else offers such perfect love and forgiveness to such undeserving people?

What the church needs above anything else is a genuine connection to the giver of life, the life the Holy Spirit brings to all who genuinely seek to dwell in the presence of God. Do we mold and shape God to be like us, to give us what we want, and to be on "our team"? Do we like the *idea* of a god, a god of our own fabrication, a god controlled by rules and traditions? When we read God's Word, do we read our own wants and desires into Scripture, molding it to fit with our lives, or do we mold our lives to fit with Scripture? Life comes when we stop trying to make Jesus like us and we start trying to make ourselves like Jesus, when we lay down our wants and desires and seek to conform everything we are and have to be like Him.

Chapter Two

INFECTED

One of the creepier zombie movies I have seen is *28 Days Later*.[1] In the movie, genetic experiments are responsible for a disease that turns people into wild, mindless zombies. Anyone who comes in contact with the blood of an infected person also contracts the disease; they lose control of themselves and of what it means to live.

The interesting twist in this film is that the zombies were living rather than undead people. They are just "sick." And that's the comparison I would like to draw here—Zombie churches aren't dead, merely sick. This speaks of hope. Unfortunately, another parallel can be drawn too: the infection is contagious and can be spread through contact. (There is comfort in the fact that the infection can be cured, but we'll arrive at that point later.)

Zombie churches aren't dead, merely sick.

Dinner with Mr. and Mrs. Zombie

I had a college friend whose parents came into town one weekend and wanted to take us to dinner. When we were seated at the restaurant, they began talking. They seemed like good people. They talked about how they went to church and all the spiritual things they did. I found myself uncomfortable. Over the course of the meal, they talked about all the things they believed to be wrong with our country as well as all of the "stupid" decisions our leadership was making.

I have to be honest: their complaints seemed petty. I had no desire to enter the conversation, but after a long silence, they put me on the spot. The father asked outright, "What do you think about all of this?" I tried to avoid responding, but he pressed for an answer.

I had recently been looking at some world statistics, and so I shared what I had learned about the needs of the world. I told them that three billion people live on less than three dollars a day. I talked about the children suffering and dying from diseases. I talked about the children starving to death. My conclusion was that we, while living in a land of luxury, ought to be more concerned with those who have nothing than with our own comforts. I wasn't trying to sound hyperspiritual. I just knew that I sometimes need to be reminded of what is really important, and I figured they did too. Their response, however, was a bit unexpected.

The father looked me in the eyes and said, "Who cares about that? We need to fix our country before we worry about anyone else." Perhaps he was right. I don't want to be one of those guys who is so concerned for people across the ocean that I neglect the people across the street, but here's what I heard: "Once I have all the comforts and luxuries I can stand, then I will worry about those in need."

I looked around the table to see both my friend and her mother nodding in agreement. Their whole family felt that we should be more concerned with a tax that made shoes a little more expensive than we should be about the starving children of the world who have never even owned a pair of shoes. These people were Christians and they seemed more concerned with taxes than with people—poor people. People whom Jesus loves.

There's a special place in the heart of God for lost and hurting people. As His children we should care for those people whom Jesus loves.

When we can hear of the suffering of others and not be affected by it, then something in the church has been lost. From that point on, I started to notice many "Christians" who seemed to have lost or forgotten the true meaning of the name amidst rituals and routines. The worst of them was the man I saw in the mirror every morning.

The title *Christian* was first given to the church in Antioch in Acts 11. It appears that the name was given to the church by those outside of the church. In fact, in its three uses in the New Testament, the term *Christian* was used exclusively by outsiders and not by Christians themselves.[2] Those outside of the church viewed Jesus as nothing more than a failed revolutionary put to death on a cross. The church had made itself look so much like Jesus that outsiders saw His followers as little versions of Him. It is possible that this term was used like an insult: "Oh, you are just one of those little Jesus followers." *Jesus freak.*

Christian means "belonging to Christ" and was a title given in reflection of how the church lived.

For whatever reason, the church grabbed hold of this title and turned it into a self-designation.[3] Christian means "belonging to Christ" and was a title given in reflection of how the church lived. This is not to say that the early church was perfect. Clearly, when we read the letters of Paul, we see they had problems just like we do. The difference is that the early church had something so special, so unorthodox, so powerful that they turned the world upside down. The early church had something that affected the way they lived so much so that outsiders started thinking of them as imitations of Jesus. Oh, to live such a life as to be thought of like that!

Devotion or Decay

In the book of Acts, Luke repeatedly points out, "the Lord added to their number daily." That seems to be the goal. Many churches genuinely desire growth; we just don't always want to make the sacrifices necessary to make that happen. We don't always want to live with a fanatical devotion to God. We want Christianity to be our belief system, a security blanket that gives us the comfort of eternal security without the expectation of anything in return.

Take the way we pray, for example. It sometimes seems like we want God to be a genie in a bottle. Sometimes we pray asking God to do everything for us and then expect it will just magically happen. We pray for patience and want to wake up a more patient person. We pray for wisdom and expect that God will just download it into our heads. We just want to put it on the Almighty Santa's list and wake up with it under the tree. Then when God puts us in a situation where we can learn the very things we asked Him for, we get upset. We don't want to have to work at it; we just want God to make it happen. I know I've tried to use Him like this.

I have used prayer as a tool to try to manipulate God into giving me what I want. I've negotiated with God so many times I lost count. "God, if You just give me this car, I will read my Bible for an hour every day for a year." "God, if You will fix this mess I made, I will pray more." I have tried to make my faith a spiritual investment where I get as much out of it as I can while putting in as little as possible. Ever done that? This attitude degrades the church. Oftentimes we show up looking for what we get, not what we have to give up.

Erwin McManus, in his book *The Barbarian Way*, says this of faith:

> Instead of finding confidence to live as we should regardless of our circumstances, we have used it as justification to choose the path of least resistance, least difficulty, least sacrifice. Instead of concluding it is best to be wherever God wants us to be, we have decided that wherever it is best for us to be is where God wants us. Actually, God's will for us is less about our comfort than it is about our contribution. God would never choose for us safety at the cost of significance.[4]

We don't desire unreasonable devotion. We don't even seem to value it. We hear stories of people like Jim Elliot who traveled with a team to minister to one of the most dangerous tribes in South America. Every one of them knew this tribe had killed all the foreigners who had come to them. They knew this was a possible, if not likely, result of their mission. They chose to go anyway. Before they were ever able to preach the gospel, they were speared to death by the tribe they came to save.[5] We read this story and say, "Wow. That is crazy. I could never do that."

Brother Birbal (not his real name) is a preacher in India. There, Christians are an unpopular minority often persecuted by the Hindus in power. One day Brother Birbal was asked to come and preach at a church. When he arrived, Hindu guards stationed inside the building held AK-47s. The preacher came to him and said, "I am so sorry. We had no idea they were going to be here this week. If you would like, we can reschedule you to come preach another time when the guards are not here." The preacher paused for a moment, but there was no response so he continued: "If you still want to preach, you can, but you should know these guards are devout Hindus. They hate Jesus, and if you say something that upsets them, they might kill you."

Passion has been replaced with cowardice and reason.

The preacher went on to explain that he had a car pulled up in the back with a driver waiting. Brother Birbal could preach if he wanted, and then if he noticed the guards were getting upset, he could run out the back door, and the driver would take him to safety. Sounds reasonable. If I were preaching at gunpoint, I might like to know there was an exit strategy.

Birbal didn't even consider this option, though. "Oh, I'm going to preach, and you can move your car because there is no way I'm getting shot in the back for the gospel."

In America, once the epicenter of the Christian faith, this boldness has been lost. Men like Brother Birbal will boldly preach in front of hostile guards armed with automatic weapons, while we cower before amiable coworkers armed with ballpoint pens. Passion has been replaced with cowardice and reason.

Play it safe.

Don't rock the boat.

Look before you leap.

Be careful.

Hedge your bets.

We say things like this because people who are willing to die for something seem crazy to those who live for nothing. The undead never really understand the living. We tend to condition people in the church to conform, to play nice. When we discourage all-out devotion for clever reason, we exchange the heart of disciples who seek the kingdom more than their own life for the heart of consumers whose primary concern is their own well-being. We frown on unpredictability, and above all, we treat people who have an unreasonable faith as religious nut jobs.

The Power of One

What we need are more people like Jonathan. Not the best-known Bible character, Jonathan is mostly known only as David's friend or Saul's son. But Jonathan has a tale of his own that is truly amazing. As Israel began to develop as an independent nation, one of their earliest opponents was the Philistines. The Philistines were seafarers, probably from Greece, who invaded from the west and settled along the southern coast of Canaan, later called Israel. The name often used to designate this area today, Palestine, likely derives from the name of this people called the Philistines.[6] We see them as a threat during the time of the judges as they fought against Samson, then King Saul, and eventually King David.

The Philistines occupied the southwest coast of Canaan from 1200–600 B.C. They seemed to be content with the land they controlled until they felt the Israelites becoming a threat, and then they rose up to crush this enemy. It is likely the threat of the Philistine forces that prompted Israel to ask God for a king. So God gave Israel King Saul. Early in his reign, Saul began an expedition to expand Israel's territory. In the process, he attacked and conquered the Philistine outpost at Geba. The Philistines didn't like this. So they sent out three retaliatory raiding parties in efforts to scatter Saul's army before battle. This tactic was pretty effective, and left Saul's army with only six hundred men. The real story, however, is not about Saul but his son Jonathan:

> On each side of the pass that Jonathan intended to cross to reach the Philistine outpost was a cliff; one was called Bozez, and the other Seneh. One cliff stood to the north toward Micmash, the other to the south toward Geba.
>
> Jonathan said to his young armor-bearer, "Come, let's go over to the outpost of those uncircumcised fellows. Perhaps the LORD will act in our behalf. Nothing can hinder the LORD from saving, whether by many or by few."
>
> "Do all that you have in mind," his armor-bearer said. "Go ahead; I am with you heart and soul."
>
> Jonathan said, "Come, then; we will cross over toward the men and let them see us. If they say to us, 'Wait there until we come to you,' we will stay where we are and not go up to them. But if they say, 'Come up to us,' we will climb up, because that will be our sign that the LORD has given them into our hands." (1 Sam. 14:4–10)

In the shadow of a coming battle, Israel found itself in a dire situation. Not only was Israel significantly outnumbered, but in the entire camp there were only two swords, one held by King Saul and the other by his son Jonathan. The Philistines apparently had removed all the Israelite blacksmiths from the land so the Hebrew fighting men would have no weapons. Perhaps the Philistines had allowed Saul and Jonathan to have swords as a special exception, but they were the only two. Saul and his six hundred remaining men were hiding. The armies of God were too afraid to stand up and fight, so they hid, waiting for something to happen.

Now the main camp of the Philistines was at Micmash, but a squad of soldiers had gone out to guard the pass that led to the Philistines' camp. That's when Jonathan said to his armor-bearer, "Let's go up and meet the Philistines." Jonathan has a strange confidence in the Lord. His statement is incredibly powerful: "Nothing can stop the Lord from saving, whether by many or by few."

God does not need armies to win battles. . . . God just looks for one person bold enough to act.

Not content to sit back and wait for a miracle, Jonathan took the initiative. He knows that when he fights, he fights with God on his side and has nothing to fear. God does not need armies to win battles. He just looks for one: one person willing to stand up, one person willing to step out in faith, one person to believe. God just looks for one person bold enough to act. So Jonathan puts his trust in the Lord, and he goes out with one sword to face the armies of the Philistines. Jonathan did not get a vision from God; he has no promise God *will* deliver him. He has no guarantee God will keep him alive. All he knows is that God is with him and that God *can* provide.

And we mustn't overlook the armor-bearer. Jonathan has a sword; the armor-bearer has . . . nothing. No weapon, no means of defending himself. Why does he agree to follow Jonathan? What is he really going to accomplish? I wish we knew this guy's name, because he deserves to be remembered as more than just Jonathan's armor-bearer. He charged a squad of well-armed, well-trained Philistine soldiers without so much as a dagger to fight with. Jonathan is courageous, certainly, but at least he had a sword. These two men were unwilling to accept things the way they were. They should be the standard of the church. All mature Christians should live with a faith like this.

Most of the soldiers had deserted or defected. The few who remained were armed with farming equipment against a foe of greater number, better training, and far superior weaponry. Hope was fading as the forces stacked up against Israel overwhelmingly. Then Jonathan attacked a Philistine outpost. He and his armor-bearer killed some twenty fully armed Philistine soldiers. Panic struck the whole army of the Philistines, and they began to scatter. By the time Saul could assemble his men, they found the Philistines in total confusion and striking each other with swords. When the soldiers of Israel who had hidden to save their lives heard the Philistines were on the run, they mustered their courage and gave chase. God delivered Israel that day because Jonathan had the faith to act without a guarantee he would survive. His boldness sparked the courage of a nation, and they rose up to fight. His actions saved the nation of Israel from almost certain destruction.

We are often like Saul and the Israelite soldiers. We are hiding in the woods when we should be charging the enemy. We wait for God to give us promises and assurances. We want a certainty of safety before we are willing to act. We need courage in our churches again. We need the courage to reach out of the box, to step out on a maybe, and to stand up for what we believe in. There is no courage in waiting for a guarantee; courage only exists where there is risk. It should be enough for us to know that God *can* deliver us even if we do not know that God *will*.

Following God does not mean we live without consequences or that those consequences will always be good. When you take a stand for Jesus, you might lose your job, you might lose friends, you might alienate your family, and one day you might even be beaten or thrown in prison. You even might die. The faith hall of fame in Hebrews 11 tells the stories of men and women who were miraculously rescued from death. This is to set the standard for our faith, however, not the standard for God's response.

We can try to make religion safe by hiding in the woods, but that only makes us undead; to truly live we must face God's expectations of faith and courage regardless of personal consequences. Our effort to preserve our life, to hide, is sometimes the very act that endangers it.

> Then Jesus said to his disciples, "If anyone would come after me, he must deny himself and take up his cross and follow me. For whoever wants to save his life will lose it, but whoever loses his life for me will find it." (Matt. 16:24–25)

Transform!

Following Jesus requires us to accept a certain degree of unknown risk. We have to be ready for the unexpected, because Jesus cares about redeeming people's souls for eternity more than He cares about temporary comforts. His trip to Golgotha proves this.

How much does your church resemble the early church in Acts?

We hide inside the four walls of the church and wonder why we don't have the same effect on the world that Jesus did. Or we work so hard to fit in that we make ourselves easy to ignore. Jesus was never easy to ignore. In the Gospels we constantly see people drawn to Jesus. Even when they do not follow Him and even when they do not accept Him, they are drawn to Him. God's desire is not to conform us but to transform us (Rom. 12:2).[7] Make no mistake, His transformation creates a dynamic life.

How much does your church resemble the early church in Acts? The early church was a group of revolutionaries who challenged the ethics and customs of the world in which they lived. The early church was noted for turning the world on its head. The early church changed the world. The modern American church has instead been changed by the world. We have been so successful at blending in that it's difficult to even tell the difference between a Christian and a non-Christian, the living from the dead. What makes it worse, we take pride in that, as if being stealth Christians was something that would impress God. The church was designed to be God's redemptive agent in the world, but that's not what we're doing. Instead of becoming a powerful force of change, we've become a costume party, a masquerade ball. Everyone dances around in their undead masks that prevent you from really knowing who they are. We make ourselves look alive. We act alive, and yet that's not always the case. The religious leaders of Jesus' day were professional actors. They put on a good show, but their hearts were not right. They looked good on the outside, but inside they were full of wickedness and evil. When we show up at church on Sunday morning wearing our best smiles and the façade that everything is perfect, aren't we doing the same thing?

Here's my caveat: I don't want to sound like I'm bashing the church. I entered the ministry for a reason, and I've stayed in the ministry for a reason. The church has its share of problems. At the same time, the church offers something that can't be found elsewhere: godly community. The church meets one of the core needs of every human being in a way that no other community really can. The church is a place where diversity can come together in harmony and we can experience facets of who God is through our relationships with other Christians that we would have never known on our own.

When I was in high school, I suffered from severe depression. I had very few friends and a nonexistent social life. I was made fun of at work, at school, and even at church. The teenagers in my youth group were the worst. For several years I felt worthless. I felt unlovable, that no one would accept me. I was mad at God for leaving me all alone in a world so cruel. One night I nearly ended my own life. Thankfully, the presence of God showed up, and I didn't go through with it. Then my family started going to a new church. I still remember sitting in the foyer expecting to be ignored like I was everywhere else in my life, when a kid from the youth group came over and invited me to his house after church. He didn't know me. He didn't have to do that. For some reason he accepted me for who I was as if that were as natural as breathing.

I'm alive today because a church community that had life offered me acceptance as I was.

The church gets it wrong sometimes . . . OK, maybe it gets things wrong a lot. Despite all that, when it gets things right, it's amazing. I'm alive today because a church community that had life offered me acceptance as I was. The church is not perfect, but it has so much to offer that we cannot give up on it.

I believe in the church. I believe that God gave us the church for a reason, and I love the church. At the same time, I look at the church in America today and I just wonder if maybe God had something more in mind. Perhaps we are not reaching our full potential. Now I believe with all my heart that there is a cure for the infection that seems to have spread through so many churches in America, but in order to accept the cure we need to first see and understand the problem.

Part of the Problem

I do not want to sound like a critic. I realize that I myself am part of the problem. I am not the hero of this story. I am writing this because I recently realized that I was the villain. I thought that I needed to organize the church and turn it into a well-oiled machine. I wrote hundreds of pages of guidelines and policies and expounded on all these subtle nuances of what a church should be. You know where that got me? Tired and frustrated. I was trying to make the church work instead of trying to connect the church to the One who loves her.

Churches that have contracted *zombiism* are not full of "bad" people but people who, like me, didn't realize the problem until they were already a part of it. I know what it is like to just go through the motions. I did it for years. In my first three years of ministry, I created a Zombie church. The fault was mine. When I came to the church, the church had just been through a really rocky patch in its history where it nearly split. It had gone from four hundred members to about forty within a few months. The people trusted me to lead them to a closer relationship with God, but I led them to stagnation. I didn't give them a vision; I didn't give them a purpose. I didn't give the church the life it needed. The people were longing for something to do, and all I gave them were sermons. I wondered why so many people came for a few weeks, then disappeared. I made excuses over and over again: "We are not ready." "We need to get ourselves taken care of and set our foundation right before we go out into the world." I made one excuse after another because I was undead and didn't really know how to be alive. The church was hungry for more, but I couldn't give it to them. I couldn't because I didn't have it myself.

Jesus isn't looking for people who have the right password. He is gathering disciples.

Then I heard a sermon by Jon Weece from Southland Christian Church. He spoke about how the church would be remembered. I started to think. What have I done to make a difference in the world? What have I done in my life that has meaning? I was reminded of a sermon a friend of mine had preached on the kingdom of God. In that moment I woke up. I looked around and realized I might as well be a zombie. I may have personally connected with the source of life, but I had built myself into a bunker and wasn't sharing it. Zombies are dead creatures that act like the living. I was a living creature acting like the dead. I had fallen into habits, rituals, and religious behavior. Something was missing, something that mindlessly jumping through the motions didn't give me. I had life but I was lacking *aliveness*. I had life but I wasn't really living it.

Our mission is to take life to a dying world. We can only do that if we have life ourselves. Jesus isn't looking for people who have the right password. He is gathering disciples: people who will share in the life that He offers by receiving it *and* living in it.

Perhaps a better title for this book would have been *Confessions of a Zombie Pastor.* I was missing my connection to the source of life, and so I wasn't leading anyone else to it. I reflected on the church events I'd initiated. They had all been for the wrong reasons. We did things just to do them because that is what you are supposed to do. We had programs with no purpose, ministries with no mission, and plans with no passion. We existed to exist.

Not long ago, some close friends of mine started up a prayer group at their local church. They met together once a week at the church to pray for each other and for the church. They got a little more "charismatic" than the church was comfortable with, so the church stopped them from meeting in the building. Then the church said they should not meet and forbade anyone in leadership from being involved in this group. When that didn't deter this group from praying, the church began to blame all their problems on them until the people became so alienated that they left the church. It sounds unbelievable, I know. If I had not witnessed it myself, I wouldn't believe it.

A church going to war with a prayer group makes no sense. The prayer group respected the authority of the church leaders, they prayed for the church leaders, and they did everything the church leaders asked them to. They were not divisive, spreading dissension, or creating disunity. All they wanted to do was to meet together and to pray, but the church leaders felt threatened by this group. Their prayers had power, and people started to get interested.

The church leaders felt their control slipping away, so they waged war on the prayer group. The leaders said that what the prayer group was doing didn't fit with the traditions of the church. *Get in line or get out.* (Can't you just picture the unrelenting forward march of a shoulder-to-shoulder line of zombies, either overtaking the living or forcing them to retreat?)

Zombie churches have permeated our entire Christian culture, not just one branch of the faith. We have become lazy in our faith. This problem transcends denomination, age, gender, background, and race. As social pressure toward Christian conformity de-radicalizes us, making us safe, comfortable, and predictable, we lose the very essence of the purpose of our existence. We do not live to fit into some spiritual mold. We live to bring people to life. When we become more concerned about offending people than about transforming people, we have lost what it means to be Christian. Too much focus on comfort or conformity makes us spiritually sterile.

As we tame new generations of Christians, we make more copies of the same problem. The call of God is to a fanatical mission that requires fanatic devotion. When you answer the call of God, you answer to no man. God's call is not to enslave you with laws and regulations but to send you out like an arsonist to a flammable world. When we make it something less, we take God out of it.

Maintaining Our Connection to Life

The underlying problem in the church today is that we seek God in the wrong places. We focus on things *about* God and miss God. This is nothing new. Religious people have struggled with this since before the establishment of the church.

> And the Father who sent me has himself testified concerning me. You have never heard his voice nor seen his form, nor does his word dwell in you, for you do not believe the one he sent. You diligently study the Scriptures because you think that by them you possess eternal life. These are the Scriptures that testify about me, yet you refuse to come to me to have life. (John 5:37–40)

We are looking for Jesus in all the wrong places. Doctrine is very important but doctrine is not God. The Bible is very important but, again, it is not God. Sometimes in the church we look for life in these places, but that is not where life is found. Even within the church, with our best intentions, we sometimes make ourselves into Pharisees by putting the words about Jesus before Jesus Himself. Many churches focus so much on what is said in Scripture that they do not seem to know Jesus at all. It is not difficult for us to turn the Bible into an idol, especially if we read it for the knowledge it gives us rather than the relationship that it builds. Life is not about what you know, it is about who you know. It comes from Jesus, plain and simple. Yet sometimes we choose to stop only at an intellectual understanding because, well, quite frankly it is easier to learn information than it is to build genuine relationship. According to author Mark Virkler,

> It is quite easy to acquire the correct doctrine and head knowledge from Scripture. We can learn what the Word says about Christ and become satisfied with that information. But such intellectual exercise does not profit our spirits at all. We must take a further step of loving trust in Jesus as a Person Who is alive

> right now and yearns to be a part of our lives. Only through heart faith can we experience the things that the Scriptures testify about Him.[8]

When we make Christianity about rules and routines, we destroy relationship. The church moves from being a revolutionary, world-changing force to being a lazy social club that exists to keep on existing. It is not uncommon for churches in America to become more like businesses than ministries. Churches spend a large portion of their time worrying about money, attendance, and customer satisfaction. They look for what is popular instead of what is right, and sometimes we are more concerned with getting by than with ministering to the lost people of the world. When we lose that sense of utter devotion, we become zombies.

Zombie metaphor aside, in John chapter 6 after Jesus feeds the five thousand, the crowds follow Him to the other side of the lake where He tells them that they must eat His flesh and drink His blood. Four times in this chapter Jesus says that His followers must eat His flesh (vv. 53, 54, 56, and 57). Most English translations just say "eats" each time. In the Greek, after the first time Jesus says "eats," a more descriptive word is used: first it's to eat, but then it's to chew, to hungrily gnaw upon, to ravenously crunch and munch as if seeking to devour.[9]

This statement would have scandalized the Jews: cannibalism was strictly forbidden in their culture because of the Law. The idea Jesus is getting at is of course not literal. He is driving toward the intensity and passion with which His followers should pursue Him. A nice light connection to Jesus will not satisfy His true followers. One encounter and they will become ravenous in their pursuit of Him. Perhaps it is best to view what Jesus said about eating His flesh and drinking His blood in light of the Sermon on the Mount: those who hunger and thirst for righteousness will be blessed (Matt. 5:6). Hunger is a strong physical desire that drives us to pursue a means of satisfying that desire and is a fitting parallel to how Christians should respond to Jesus.

What Jesus said to the crowd was shocking and offensive. The Jews had important laws about clean and unclean foods, and a religious teacher saying to eat His flesh would have scandalized the lot of them. Of course, Jesus was not speaking literally, but what *did* He mean? I believe He meant that we must accept Him on the deepest levels. We have to allow Jesus to permeate all that we do in our daily lives, from the way we talk, to our work and our rest, to how we live and love. Jesus is not just a person you believe in. Having the life He offers comes from being united with Him down to the core of who you are. In that union there is a powerful life that restores what has been lost. Failing to maintain this deep connection prevents us from fully having the life Jesus intended.

Chapter Three

THE TRANSFORMATION PROCESS

In the movie *28 Days Later,*[1] people who were infected transformed into zombies when the blood of a sick person came in contact with their blood, eyes, or mouth. As the movie develops, the main character, Jim, befriends a father and his daughter with whom he travels, trying to find a safe place to live. While they are traveling, a drop of polluted blood happens to splatter into the father's eye. He tries to blink it out but it is too late. He realizes that he is starting to change and there is nothing that can be done. He yells at Jim to get his daughter away from him as he slowly begins to lose control of his body. He tries to ensure his daughter's safety as he is transformed into the very monsters they were trying to escape.

The transformation from living to undead can happen very quickly. One minute everything seems fine, the next you are a fiendish member of the not-so-deceased club.

Imagine following a guide through the woods at night. It wouldn't take much for you to lose sight of him. In fact, if you took your eyes off him for even a moment, you could become totally lost. When the Holy Spirit moves, if we don't move with Him, then the transformation begins. It's not too many steps without the Spirit before the church is totally lost.

The church is ever, only, always about Jesus.

Every church thinks their way of doing church is right, that they have cornered the market on *life*. But life comes from God, not from our religious routines. What every church must do is keep their eyes on the Spirit. Maybe He wants to disrupt our religious routines. Maybe He is leading your church to a stylistic change that would increase the church's ability to minister to a younger, less traditional audience. Maybe He is leading your church to a more (dare I say) traditional approach, to teach that same young audience how to connect with practices that have gone on for thousands of years. The point is, when the Spirit is moving, are you willing to pull up stakes and follow Him? Are you willing to sacrifice your own comfort in order to be closer to the Holy Spirit?

Church is not about us. It is not about our wants. It is not about our needs. It is not about our preferences. The church is ever, only, always about Jesus. Methods may change but the message never will. A church that is not driven by the Spirit of God and centered completely on Jesus is a church that will be devoid of genuine life.

The Infection of Laziness

When we think of laziness, we picture the grown man who still lives in his parents' basement. Or the woman whose most pressing engagement is a manicure. The person who accomplishes little or nothing in life.

I have met some lazy people in my life. I knew a guy once who was proud of the fact that he did not shower for over two weeks. And there was the guy who worked a guard job where he could play on the computer or sleep all night, and then came home and did the same. Some people go to extraordinary lengths to do as little work as possible. I heard of one guy who had gotten married, and he and his wife were constantly asking the church for financial help. He admitted to people that his plan was to draw unemployment through the winter and to look for a job in the spring. He made plans to not work or even look for a job because he could get paid to do nothing for months at a time. Call me old-fashioned, but I find this attitude unbelievable.

When Jesus comes to us, He is inviting us to follow Him. To go where He goes, to do what He does, to be where He is. The commission He gives us to follow is a dynamic demand. He is not inviting us along for a nice walk along the beach on a divine vacation. The natural expectation in following Jesus is that you will serve and work for Him. If you came along for a fun ride or to get away from work, then the God you are looking for isn't Jesus and isn't real. Following Jesus is a commission to serve—to work—in His field. We ought to think of following Him more like enlisting than like a social club membership. Christianity is not a system of beliefs; it is a lifestyle.

When we work for God and not for men, we realize that our best is still not enough. That is the beauty of the grace of God. We can't earn salvation, and He doesn't let us. God does for us what we could never do for ourselves: He takes away our sins. God has given us something so great that sitting back and doing nothing is not an appropriate response. We must not be idle in our faith, for an idle Christian is hardly a Christian at all. Idleness is not just a busyness issue; it is a heart issue.

I was in my office one day when a car pulled up to the church. A couple stepped out and came inside to speak with me. They explained how they needed money for food so they could feed their kids. While we were talking, I happened to look outside and see their car. They were driving a brand-new Lexus with tinted windows, chrome rims, and a nice sunroof. Their car cost more than the values of the cars of our entire staff put together plus my yearly salary, yet these people wanted us to give them food. *Yeah, if I bought that car, I would have to find some food pantries as well,* I thought. Then it hit me, again. This was not a reflection of the heart of Jesus. I was judging people based on what I saw because it was easier to judge them than it was care for them. I thought they were lazy, when really I was the lazy one. Paul wrote on this issue of laziness:

> In the name of the Lord Jesus Christ, we command you, brothers, to keep away from every brother who is idle and does not live according to the teaching you received from us. For you yourselves know how you ought to follow our example. We were not idle when we were with you, nor did we eat anyone's food without paying for it. On the contrary, we worked night and day, laboring and toiling so that we would not be a burden to any of you. We did this, not because we do not have the right to such help, but in order to make ourselves a model for you to follow. For even when we were with you, we gave you this rule: "If a man will not work, he shall not eat."
>
> We hear that some among you are idle. They are not busy; they are busybodies. Such people we command and urge in the Lord Jesus Christ to settle down and earn the bread they eat. And as for you, brothers, never tire of doing what is right.
>
> If anyone does not obey our instruction in this letter, take special note of him. Do not associate with him, in order that he may feel ashamed. Yet do not regard him as an enemy, but warn him as a brother. (2 Thess. 3:6–15)

Paul is not just stating an opinion but invoking the name of Jesus to give authority to this command. He creates a sense of urgency. This isn't just an idea from a church leader but a command from the Lord: avoid all of those who remain idle. This idleness may take the form of physical laziness or, as it did in my case, spiritual laziness.

Laziness is the sin of neglecting our responsibilities. By this definition, lazy people are those who fail to do what they *should do.* So you can be busy and lazy at the same time. Thus this infection of laziness is not just about how much work we accomplish but where our priorities really lie. Most of us are unaware of just how dangerous laziness is because it doesn't seem like laziness hurts anyone.

Laziness is the sin of neglecting our responsibilities.

The church used to make demands of people, but over the years the church has gotten away from that. The fear of turning someone away and hurting the weekly attendance average seems to have overruled our desire to remain obedient to the Word of God. When we support people who are not active in their faith, we enable them to remain lazy. We frequently neglect passages like this one in 2 Thessalonians in which the church is told to disciple people on how they live.

Our churches become little businesses fighting to keep their customers happy.

Paul first works on those whose hearts are in the right place. He tells them to keep doing what is right. In living a proper Christian life, the actions of a Christian should naturally shame and challenge those who are idle. The hope would be that in seeing the activity of those who have a genuine relationship with God, those who are sitting on the sidelines will be inspired to follow their example.

The idle are not to be expelled from the community as the immoral who call themselves Christians but do not live accordingly should be, but they are certainly to be denied some of the privileges that come from being an active part of the church. Today our perspective seems backward. With all the churches available, we have begun to believe that the church is blessed to have people join. Our churches become little businesses fighting to keep their customers happy. "We cannot do that even though it is a good idea because some people won't like it, and if they don't like it, they will leave and go to another church down the street and we will lose their tithe."

In a consumer-based culture, we seem to have created a consumer-based church that focuses not so much on the truth of God but on pleasing its members. With this consumer mind-set, everything the church does reverts back to what makes the people happy or what the wealthy donors want. So we tolerate idlers rather than confront them.

We forget that idleness can have an adverse effect. At a work site or in a business environment, idle workers cause problems. They are a burden on others, using resources while contributing nothing in return. They are a distraction to others and often occupy their time with gossip, slander, or meddling. And they are a temptation to others, as their laziness, like a toxic fume, quickly infects the entire area and leads others to stop working.

Christians are expected to live out their faith and have a responsibility to do so. Those who carry out this responsibility and are living obedient Christian lives are commanded by God to avoid the "dead weight" Christians who don't do anything. Basically, the undead contaminate the living. We must remember to treat them with the love of God while keeping enough distance that we do not become infected ourselves. We must maintain the relationship for the purpose of restoration, that they may see our lives and follow our example. The key to this is balance. We must not be so distant that they feel unloved or disconnected, but not become so close that their lifestyle begins to affect ours.

Dedication or Destruction

A few years ago, I counseled a couple who were going through some serious marriage problems. The husband had been going out to bars after work, getting drunk, and flirting. He found one woman to be more attractive than his wife and was honestly considering having an affair with her. As we talked, I perceived that he was emotionally disconnected from his wife. The problem was, he had started taking her for granted. He had stopped investing in their relationship, so they were drifting apart. With space between them, there was the opportunity for temptation. He knew how to love his wife. He knew how to romance and to treat her well. He had simply neglected to do so. Thankfully he realized the need to go home and do more than just watch TV. He needed to serve his wife. In doing so, the flame of their marriage was reignited.

Laziness inevitably destroys our relationships with others, and our relationship with God.

Laziness inevitably destroys our relationships with others, and our relationship with God. Most relationships do not end because the couple was inherently incompatible. The problem is, when the initial excitement wears off, people get comfortable, selfish, and lazy. This is true in all of our relationships. We know we *ought* to treat our spouses with honor, our co-workers with respect, our friends with kindness, our God with reverence. We know what we *should* do; we just neglect to do it. I believe the reason we like to turn a relationship with God into a mechanical routine is that then it requires less effort. Relationships demand . . . everything.

The danger of spiritual laziness is that it corrupts the atmosphere and function of the church.[2] Those who do not do, talk. Idle talkers begin to speak of things that do not matter. This idle or careless speech is offensive to God (Matt. 12:36; James 1:26; 1 Tim. 5:13). As we begin to trade action for words, we display our own hypocrisy. Often the fruit of idleness is disunity and division. Spiritual laziness comes from neglecting the commission we have been given by God. It is what we often do in our local churches: we show up and we leave, but we don't take Jesus with us.

In the parable of the talents, the lazy servant is called wicked (Matt. 25:26; Luke 19:22). He was not expecting his master to return, and he lived accordingly. We are not called to warm chairs. We are not called to live a comfortable life. We are not called to simply sing songs of praise once or twice a week. We are called to service in the kingdom God. The Christian life is not about what you claim. It is about what you believe. True belief cannot be separated from what we do.

If I told you I was going to buy you a new car and all you needed to do was to go to the dealership and pick out whatever car you wanted, if you believed me, you would go—and right now. You would put this book down and rush to the dealership to select your car before I changed my mind. The reason you are still reading this is because you don't actually believe that I'm going to buy you a car. What you do is determined by what you believe.

> They claim to know God, but by their actions they deny him. They are detestable, disobedient and unfit for doing anything good. (Titus 1:16)

The laziness that exists in our spiritual lives can be seen in the amount of time we spend wondering about how much we need to do to be saved. When we look for some minimum standard of God, we're not seeking to glorify God. We're bargain shopping. We're trying to ensure our entry into heaven at the lowest possible price. Scripture is very clear that we are saved by the grace of God through faith and not by works (Eph. 2:8–9). By thinking that there is any amount, however minimal, of stuff you can "do" to be saved, you reduce salvation to a works-based reward system rather than accepting God's grace as a free gift—a free gift that we are afraid will end up being too costly. In doing so, we separate faith from action.

The noteworthy thing about the men and women of faith all throughout history isn't so much the clever, philosophical things they said but what they did. Words might be remembered, but the people we remember are people who did something. Words without actions are vacuous. The big difference between the semblance of life that exists in Zombie churches and the genuine life of a follower of Jesus is the missing verbs. As James says:

> In the same way, faith by itself, if it is not accompanied by action, is dead.
>
> But someone will say, "You have faith; I have deeds." Show me your faith without deeds, and I will show you my faith by what I do. You believe that there is one God. Good! Even the demons believe that—and shudder.
>
> You foolish man, do you want evidence that faith without deeds is useless? (James 2:17–20)

The point is not to say that we earn our salvation by what we do. Yet what good is faith if it doesn't affect the way we live? If you believe you are sick, you go to a doctor. If you believe your friend is in need, you go help. Belief is not isolated from action, it dictates our actions. When we fail to act, it is not because Jesus doesn't call us to it. It is because we don't really believe Him.

If we view faith as a mere cognitive recognition of God's existence, we can compartmentalize it, separating what we believe from how we live. In the waffle of my life, I can then tuck *faith* into one of the little boxes and leave it there. *My favorite color is blue. I believe in God. I like tacos.* The fact that I like tacos *may* affect my choice of what I have for dinner, but it doesn't have to. After all, tacos every day may get boring, and I may get sick of them. I like tacos, but that is just one aspect of who I am; it doesn't control me. My belief in God *may* affect how I talk to my neighbor, but it doesn't have to. Doing the right thing day after day seems dull. I like it when God is a part of life, but I want Him to stay in His little compartment. No. In the waffle of my life, faith has to be the syrup that covers all the little boxes and absorbs into the waffle itself. My faith cannot be contained in one little area of my life; if it is alive, then it spills over the edges and is absorbed into every area of my life.

We'll talk about this more in the coming chapters, but the point I'm making is that we cannot separate faith from actions. If we don't live for God, then the truth is we don't really believe in God.

Consider the parable Jesus tells in Matthew 20:

> For the kingdom of heaven is like a landowner who went out early in the morning to hire men to work in his vineyard. He agreed to pay them a denarius for the day and sent them into his vineyard.
>
> About the third hour he went out and saw others standing in the marketplace doing nothing. He told them, "You also go and work in my vineyard, and I will pay you whatever is right." So they went.
>
> He went out again about the sixth hour and the ninth hour and did the same thing. About the eleventh hour he went out and found still others standing around. He asked them, "Why have you been standing here all day long doing nothing?"
>
> "Because no one has hired us," they answered.
>
> He said to them, "You also go and work in my vineyard."
>
> When evening came, the owner of the vineyard said to his

> foreman, "Call the workers and pay them their wages, beginning with the last ones hired and going on to the first."
>
> The workers who were hired about the eleventh hour came and each received a denarius. So when those came who were hired first, they expected to receive more. But each one of them also received a denarius. When they received it, they began to grumble against the landowner. "These men who were hired last worked only one hour," they said, "and you have made them equal to us who have borne the burden of the work and the heat of the day."
>
> But he answered one of them, "Friend, I am not being unfair to you. Didn't you agree to work for a denarius? Take your pay and go. I want to give the man who was hired last the same as I gave you. Don't I have the right to do what I want with my own money? Or are you envious because I am generous?"
>
> So the last will be first, and the first will be last. (Matt. 20:1–16)

Clearly, the point is not how much work you have done for salvation or how long you have been a Christian, but how you use the time that you have. A person who has been a Christian for forty years should have accomplished far more for the kingdom of God than a new convert, just as the first workers hired in the vineyard should have done more work than the workers hired with only an hour left. God in His grace may decide to give them all the same reward, but the truth is the first worker should have gotten a lot more done.

Both of these groups are blessed. Those who have a relationship with Jesus for many years are blessed to know Him and to share their lives with Him. They are blessed to know that the work they do is for the glory of God and that their life has meaning and eternal significance. They get to work for the One they love. They get to recognize His provision and His grace every day.

Those who come to Jesus late do not have this same joy, at least not in the same way. What they have instead is the joy of knowing the depth of the grace of God. They may realize His love for them even more than the long-term workers because they receive the same life as the workers who have been working all day. They get the same reward even though they didn't "do as much work to get it," even if they come to Jesus on their deathbed. What a powerful realization of love.

Thus the grace and glory of God can be seen in different ways by both groups.

So what do all the people in the parable have in common? They are all workers.

> As the body without the spirit is dead, so faith without deeds is dead. (James 2:26)

This is key! None of these men were called to come, sit outside the fields, and do nothing. Those who have a living faith in Jesus Christ are workers for God's kingdom. Not because they are trying to earn their salvation, not because they feel guilt or obligation, but because their faith prompts them to work.

Motivated by Love

The cure for spiritual laziness (or any other spiritual infection) is found in proper motivation. A dead church comes alive when its people are properly motivated.

> According to the early Christians, the church doesn't exist in order to provide a place where people can pursue their private spiritual agendas and develop their own spiritual potential. Nor does it exist in order to provide a safe haven in which people can hide from the wicked world and ensure that they themselves arrive safely at an otherworldly destination. Private spiritual growth and ultimate salvation come rather as the byproducts of the main, central, overarching purpose for which God has

> called and is calling us. This purpose is clearly stated in various places in the New Testament: that through the church God will announce to the wider world that he is indeed its wise, loving, and just creator; that through Jesus he has defeated the powers that corrupt and enslave it; and that by his Spirit he is at work to heal and renew it.[3]

We can be pretty selfish in our treatment of the God who offers us everything. I am OK with praying 150 times a year, but 250 seems like a little much. We want all the blessings, all the riches, and all the treasures of heaven for eternity; what we don't want is to be bothered with doing anything in return. When we neglect the commission we were given by Jesus, we are lazy. When we sit comfortably inside the four walls of our churches while the world around us suffers and dies in darkness, we are lazy. We have access to the light of life, and we live in a world that is full of darkness. The darkness that we see is not an indication of the strength of our enemy; it is a result of our own inaction. We fail to take the light into the world, and as a result, it remains in darkness.

The darkness that we see is not an indication of the strength of our enemy; it is a result of our own inaction.

If motivation is the key to solving this problem of laziness, 1 Corinthians 13 gives us the cure:

> And now I will show you the most excellent way.
>
> If I speak in the tongues of men and of angels, but have not love, I am only a resounding gong or a clanging cymbal. If I have the gift of prophecy and can fathom all mysteries and all knowledge, and if I have a faith that can move mountains, but have not love, I am nothing. If I give all I possess to the poor and surrender my body to the flames, but have not love, I gain nothing.
>
> Love is patient, love is kind. It does not envy, it does not

> boast, it is not proud. It is not rude, it is not self-seeking, it is not easily angered, it keeps no record of wrongs. Love does not delight in evil but rejoices with the truth. It always protects, always trusts, always hopes, always perseveres.
>
> Love never fails. (1 Cor. 12:31–13:8)

Yet if the wrong thing motivates our love, we are in trouble as T. S. Eliot once warned against in a play through one of his characters who said: "The last temptation is the greatest treason: / To do the right deed for the wrong reason"[4] If we do the right things for the wrong reasons . . . it is still wrong. Intent always precedes content. It is not enough to go through the motions. If it were, God would not have given us a New Testament. If all we were supposed to do was follow the rules and do the right things, then Jesus' teachings don't make any sense. The point is, we must do the right things for the right reasons. It is for the love of God that we shine our light into the darkness. It is for the love of others that we risk standing up and getting beaten to show them the love of God. It is not until we love that we really understand what it means to be Christian.

Jesus calls us to love. Loving God is the greatest commandment. Loving others is second. We are also called to love the fellowship of believers—to love the church. Consider what happens when we neglect any one of the three: *Isolated zombies* love God and love others, but they abandon the church because she is full of imperfect people. *Organized zombies* love God and they love the church, but they don't love others. The way they treat those outside of their walls is almost cruel and hostile. In their churches you'll find organized groups of zombies working together to destroy the living. Finally, *liberal zombies* love the church and love others, but they neglect to teach and stand on the love of God. These are often the victims of the organized zombie attack. They have locked themselves away from God to avoid detection from the undead.

Laziness can often be the beginning of the transformation into a Zombie church. The cure for laziness is love. When you love someone, you do not sit around and do nothing, waiting for them to serve you. Love serves.

Love supports. Love works. I love my wife when I clean the house while she is out. I love my wife when I cook dinner for her. I love my wife when I run out to the store to get her something she wants. When you love someone, you act on their behalf; you will naturally do things for them. Love is an action, not just a feeling.

> Dear children, let us not love with words or tongue but with actions and in truth. (1 John 3:18)

Here's where it gets tricky. Works-based salvation is all about the work you do (actions). It is built on making yourself good enough. Grace-based salvation is based on love. You receive and you give it (actions). On the surface, these might look the similar. The dead may have the appearance of life. The two groups may do some of the same things, but while the first group is doing them because they think they have to, the second group chooses to do them because they want to share the love they have. The difference is not always found in how things look but in how they really are. Good works—prayer, reading the Bible, going to church, tithing, even serving—can be done without any love for God in our hearts. Zombies are creatures that do the same things as the living, but they do not have life; their hearts aren't in it. The difference is what's underneath. The motivation is what makes the difference. While the actions may look similar, the results are vastly different. Actions that come as a result of love bring life while good deeds done out of obligation do not.

Bombs have kill-radiuses, churches should have love-radiuses—anyone living within twenty miles of a church should know it.

When we as Christians let our light shine before men, we do the work that God has called us to do. Any church that has the light of life and does not offer it to the world is a dead or dying church. As I began to recognize that I had become a zombie pastor, I realized that most of the people living right next door to us had no idea they lived near a church. We were so distant and disconnected that people could live within five hundred yards of the church and not know it. It was time to end our slumber. Bombs have kill-radiuses, churches should have love-radiuses—anyone living within twenty miles of a church should know it.

A Church Alive

My parents go to a church in the St. Louis area, and they have people that travel over an hour and half every week to attend their church. One of the things the pastor says from time to time is that "a church alive is worth the drive." The thing is, those people shouldn't have to drive. On their Sunday morning commute, many people travel past a surprising number of churches. It is one thing to travel to attend church with some close friends or family, or even because you live in a rural area, but to have to drive that far just to find a church worth being a part of is sad.

The problem with the undead is that they don't keep to themselves.

Life should be the standard in every church, not the exception. I remember driving to take something to a friend of mine. When I turned off the highway, I drove for no more than six blocks down two little roads. I passed nine churches. At least two of the intersections had multiple churches located on it. Why? What possible benefit could there be? The only conceivable reason is because a bunch of churches want to do things "their way," even to the neglect of God's way. A church that neglects God will not stay *alive* for long.

Can a church really be a church without life? Certainly not!

So what is it?

Several factors can rob a church of its life: laziness, selfishness, pride, greed, and the like. When we are worried about personal indulgence rather than the mission God gave us, we remove life from the church by making church all about us. One thing that will inevitably kill a church is making it about anything other than Jesus.

The problem with the undead is that they don't keep to themselves.

The undead seem bent on spreading their condition to all they come in contact with. Zombie Christians are dangerous because they will spread their disease to those around them. One undead heart results in an entire undead community, and before you know it we find one more Zombie church. We must fight to prevent the spread of this terrible disease before it is too late.

Acts 12 teaches us an important lesson:

> It was about this time that King Herod arrested some who belonged to the church, intending to persecute them. He had James, the brother of John, put to death with the sword. When he saw that this pleased the Jews, he proceeded to seize Peter also. This happened during the Feast of Unleavened Bread. (Acts 12:1–3)

James, the apostle, one of Jesus' inner three, is put to death with a sword, decapitated. This is a sad day for the church. The church was growing, things were going so well, and now apostles are being arrested and killed. It is really pretty disheartening. Peter, the rock on which Christ would build His church, is in prison and it does not take a genius to guess what will happen to him. The way things are going, that might as well be death row. This doesn't seem like a good time to be a part of the church. In fact, it looks like church is about ready to fall apart.

Sometimes our lives can feel like this too. Christianity is not as easy as you thought it would be. It seemed like it offered a better life, but now, having seen all the trials and the pain, you're not so sure. You're inclined to think that the temptations in your life are too great for you to resist. You would be mistaken.

There is strength in the church. There is power for those who hold on to the kingdom of God. Let me show you something really cool. At the beginning of Acts 12, James is beheaded, Peter is in prison, and Herod is king. This does not look good for the church. But look again: by Acts 13 Herod is dead, Peter is free, and the church is alive and well.

There is a cure to our condition. It is *life*. Life is contagious and it can bring hope to an entire community. While the infection of zombie Christians has the ability to spread like a disease, healthy Christians spread life like a California wildfire. The truth is, zombiism is like darkness; it can only exist in the absence of life. The disease can spread, but only where people have drifted from the life Jesus offers. The blood of the Lamb trumps the blood of the undead every time. Even a church dominated by zombies can be transformed by a single person who has true life.

If you are alive in zombie land, you may get voted off the island, but every day you have a chance to let your light shine and to bring life to the lifeless. Make no mistake; bringing dead churches to life will be a battle, but as you will soon learn, it is a battle that can be won.

Chapter Four

THE SYMPTOMS

In the 2004 movie *Dawn of the Dead,*[1] one of the main characters, Andre, and several other survivors manage to make their way to the local mall without being turned. As they try to lock the mall down, Andre's pregnant wife gets a small bite from one of the zombies. Andre tries to pretend she is fine, although she clearly is not, and one of the other survivors freaks out and shoots him.

Zombies in our churches are like zombies in horror movies—they infect those they come in contact with.

Andre tried to ignore the symptoms. His wife was bitten, and they had no cure. He lost his own life because he refused to see the warnings.

Zombies in our churches are like zombies in horror movies—they infect those they come in contact with. Denying it won't change anything. Here we must break from the mythos a little: in most zombie movies the only "cure" is to kill the zombies. Survival in a Zombie church is not accomplished by killing off the zombies, however; it is about curing the infection.

Diseases have symptoms; this is how our body lets us know something is wrong. It is safe to assume that if there is an infection in the church, there will be symptoms. One of the most efficient church killers I have seen is worldliness. Instead of transforming, the church is conforming. In our materialistic world that prizes wealth and the accumulation of possessions, the church begins its change. She begins to take on the standards and values of the world, acting like the world rather than acting like Jesus.

The church described in the book of Acts was a self-sacrificing church where believers were selling their private possessions and property and bringing them to the apostles to distribute to those in need. We don't see a lot of that happening today. The people who had sacrificed personal comforts for the good of the community were not focused on having nice buildings or fancy lights or comfortable chairs; they just wanted to take care of people's needs. A beautiful church is not always a dying church, but sometimes external beauty masks internal decay.

Recognizing the Condition

Pain is your body's way of telling you that something is wrong. Although it's unpleasant, pain is an extremely important part of life. When your body is out of balance, it lets you know in a variety of ways. These symptoms help us identify the condition that besets us. A church that is losing its connection to life will display certain painful characteristics: bitterness, resentment, disunity, quarreling, closed-mindedness . . . Consider these life-threatening symptoms:

1. *A dying church will have idols.* Not necessarily *bad* things, an idol is anything we treat as more important than God. Communion, baptism, service, prayer, worship . . . *anything* can be an idol. One thing you will certainly see in a church that has lost its connection to life is that something, likely a religious thing, will have taken precedence over God.

2. *A dying church guards its rules and rituals.* Traditions are not evil, but when tradition is simply for the sake of tradition, it is likely a result of

the church's attempt to compensate. When the relationship with God is gone, we often try to fill that void with religious practices to feel "connected to the divine."

3. *A dying church lacks intimacy.* People in Zombie churches are often friendly but not closely connected. Close connections have a tendency to help us grow and develop in our relationship with God. As brothers and sisters in Christ encourage us to confession and repentance, we can help lead each other to restoration and faithfulness and intimacy with God.

4. *A dying church focuses inward.* Of course it is important to take care of the community within a church family. The purpose of godly community is to support and encourage each other. The danger comes not when this happens but when this is all that happens. The purpose of our encouragement and support is not so we will feel better about ourselves but so we will be better able to go back out into the world and show people Jesus.

5. *A dying church will have an unhealthy devotion to doctrine.* Sound biblical teaching is one of the most important things a church can offer. In light of the significance of doctrine, the church has in many cases crossed a line. Few people are crueler than a Christian who disagrees with your theology. They will say terrible and hateful things in the name of "preserving sound doctrine." These hypercriticals will rip people apart for not adhering to their code of conduct. Some of the most belligerent people carry extreme views on nonessential biblical issues, and if you even hint at disagreeing with them, they would all but try to revoke your Christian privileges and stamp you with the mark of the beast.

Few people are crueler than a Christian who disagrees with your theology.

In a parable about lost sheep, Jesus says, "Suppose one of you has a hundred sheep and loses one of them. Does he not leave the ninety-nine in the

What turned me into a zombie pastor was an inward focus.

open country and go after the lost sheep until he finds it?" (Luke 15:4). Shepherds tend sheep. When one gets lost they go out and look for it. When all churches do is care for the sheep that are safe, the church is failing to fully shepherd its flock.

Some Christians fear the direction our country is going and are talking of the coming persecution of the church, yet the primary danger we face is not an enemy on the outside but the enemy within. What turned me into a zombie pastor was an inward focus. I focused the attention of the church on us and not on the needs around us. When a church stops making a difference in its community, then it's probably drifting away from the Holy Spirit.

Commitment or Chaos

Answering the call of God in our lives is an extreme commitment. As Jesus said, "anyone who does not carry his cross and follow me cannot be my disciple" (Luke 14:27)—that's a call to absolute commitment. This life is not about how you start but where you finish.

Sometimes it seems as if our lives are on simmer; we've turned the heat down so low the sauce is barely warm. Jesus says, "I know your deeds, that you are neither cold nor hot. I wish you were either one or the other! So, because you are lukewarm—neither hot nor cold—I am about to spit you out of my mouth" (Rev. 3:15–16). Either be all in or don't bother getting in. Just look at the legacies of the apostles: Paul was beheaded, Peter was crucified upside down, Thomas was speared to death, James the brother of John was beheaded, Andrew and the other James were crucified, Nathanael was skinned alive and beheaded; Simon, Thaddeus, Philip, and Matthew were all martyred for their faith.[2] Of the eleven faithful disciples, John is the only one who wasn't martyred for his faith. The apostles were definitely all in.

A great portion of those who followed Jesus in the beginning were persecuted or killed for it; yet today, having a willingness to experience persecution is almost unheard of. We aren't even willing to give up our personal freedoms not to mention our lives. In the church in America, we see little persecution. Is that because God is protecting us or because we are not living in a way that motivates the world to persecute us?

I heard the story of a man living in Haiti who wanted to sell his house for two thousand dollars. Another man very much wanted to buy that house but could not come up with the money to do so. After a great deal of negotiating, the owner of the house agreed to sell for half of the asking price. He had, however, one condition. He would still own the one nail hanging over the front door to the house. The terms were accepted and the sale was complete.

A few years later, the man who had originally owned the house wanted to buy it back. The new owner refused to sell. So the first owner hung the decaying body of a dead animal on the nail over the front door, the one part of the house he still owned. It didn't take long for the odor to become so potent that the new owner couldn't stand to live there anymore, and he agreed to sell the house back to the original owner.

This is the reality of our spiritual lives. When we allow just one part to go uncommitted by holding on to control of even the seemingly smallest, most insignificant aspect of our lives, we prevent ourselves from committing. Many of us have made a partial commitment to Christ, but there are certain things we keep for ourselves. As a result our sin becomes a festering carcass over our front door. This one little area of our lives can ruin everything else.

From time to time we are all guilty of getting caught up in the appearance and ignoring the reality. Sometimes we turn ourselves into modern-day Pharisees. We fake a deep relationship with God and spiritual maturity because it's easier. We can look spiritual and maintain control of our lives. Actually being spiritual means we have to allow a force that is greater than ourselves to take control, and it means we have to really commit ourselves to something. This issue of commitment is often a symptom of churches without life.

The trends of our culture are scary. I performed a wedding for a young couple not too long ago. They had been married for about a year when the husband approached me, saying they needed help. His wife had moved in with another man. They were both regular attendees of a church and claimed to have a solid relationship with God. Yet somehow, in less than a year, their marriage had fallen apart and the wife had broken her commitment to her husband. According to surveys taken by the Barna Group, the divorce rate is still climbing and within the church is now "statistically identical to that of non-born again adults."[3]

Our relationship to the church is sort of like a marriage; it should neither be taken lightly nor discarded easily.

There is an increase in the percentage of people who will commit to an event but fail to show up for it. Most clubs or organizations are finding they are less likely to attract new members if they require a multiyear commitment. The percentage of people who are willing to join organizations, churches, unions, political parties, and community associations is declining. The percentage of people willing to fight for the country, regardless of the cause, is declining. Throughout our society, what we are seeing is an increased unwillingness to truly commit. This is why most church membership means absolutely nothing. You show up, place your membership, and can decide to leave at any point with no requirements or consequences because there is no actual commitment. Our churches are set up to accommodate such behavior. Now I am not suggesting that churches stop having membership but perhaps that some changes be made so that membership means something—some guidelines, base expectations, prerequisites to membership, some form of genuine commitment. Our relationship to the church is sort of like a marriage; it should neither be taken lightly nor discarded easily.

We need to change our attitude about church. It is more than a place to get your needs met. Church is not about you; it is about Jesus. Your involvement in a church should benefit both you and the church. When you go to church for what you can get out of it, you will be committed only insomuch as it benefits you to be. That isn't service; it's selfishness, and this takes the life right out of church. When the focus of the church, and by that I mean the people, is on something other than Jesus, then the focus is not on the source of life, and life will not be found there. Church can't be about you and about Jesus at the same time. Making church about us robs the church of life and prevents us from getting what we need from it.

Contribute to the Cure

A church without commitment is like a car without an engine. It won't take you very far. We must not forget that we will be judged for how we live our lives. Are we ready to stand before the almighty God and explain to Him the reason we accomplished so little?

Churches are not sustaining moral values, promoting truth, changing lives, or turning the world upside down. Many simply exist. Because *we* simply exist. Less than 20 percent of those who are a regular part of the church invest their time and energy into kingdom work. Less than 10 percent of all Christians tithe their income to God.[4] Our culture is built around time and money. In our relationships with God, we have failed to adequately commit either to Him.

I heard Mark Driscoll, pastor of Seattle megachurch Mars Hill, talk about their church finances one week. "Do you realize that if you give one dollar to this church, then you are giving more than one-third of our members?" he said. Amazing. We sometimes think that big churches don't have problems. He continued, "If you give two hundred dollars a year, then you are giving more than two-thirds of our members."

Two-thirds! So this church is funded almost exclusively by 33 percent of the people who go there. Tithing—giving a portion of your earnings back to God—is a basic principle of the Christian life, and yet so few Christians understand it or feel led to do it. Plenty of churches seem to have their hands out, always asking for more. The fact is, they shouldn't have to.

More than just a building, the church is a community dedicated to doing the work of God on earth.

We who are part of the church should have a sense of ownership in the church. More than just a building, the church is a community dedicated to doing the work of God on earth. That is what we are giving to. Sure, a part of that goes to pay the bills to keep the lights on, but that too contributes to impacting people's lives with the love of Jesus. It is sad when a church has bad priorities or makes bad investments. What is really depressing is to think that maybe a few extra dollars would be all it takes to reach a lost person with the love of Jesus. We have people who show up, enjoy the community, get what they need, and . . . give nothing back. They have become leeches, sapping the life of a community. They are rocks, lumps of lifeless matter that trip up and slow down the work.

What we have is not the kingdom. We have churches without funding. We have workers without commitment. We have a mission—to love a world that is lost without the message that only we have. We need people who are committed to the cause of Christ and the commission He has given us. What if we became a church that was truly committed to the cause of Christ? What if every Christian invested in the church for the good of the community and not just their own benefit? Can you imagine how powerful the church could be if godly people united together to accomplish His purpose on the earth?

The sad result of Zombie churches is not that attendance drops but that the significance and power of the church goes unrealized. There is so much untapped potential in the community of God on the earth. If we worked together in unity with the power of God on our side, there is no obstacle that could stop us, no force that could defeat us, no trial that could overwhelm us, and no wall that could contain us.

God has the power to save a nation with one Jonathan. He has the power to deliver His people with a man like Moses. He has the power to change the world with a few men like the apostles who are sold out for His kingdom. Can you imagine what God could do if entire churches lived with the devotion of the apostles? If God can change the world with one, I wonder what He could do with an entire church of committed Christians.

Jesus sets a path for us to follow, but oftentimes we miss it. How often our lives warrant the reproach of these words, engraved on a slab in the cathedral of Lübeck, Germany:

> You call me Master and obey me not. You call me Light and see me not. You call me Way and follow me not. You call me Life and desire me not. You call me Wise and acknowledge me not. You call me Fair and love me not. You call me Rich and ask me not. You call me Eternal and seek me not. You call me Gracious and trust me not. You call me Noble and serve me not. You call me Mighty and honor me not. You call me Just and fear me not. If I condemn you, blame me not.

We cannot follow, obey, love, or seek God without a commitment to Him. We have to be willing to set aside everything else. We have plenty of commentators on the church, plenty of critics who sit on the sidelines and point out all its flaws, who try to prove their "intellectual prowess" by criticizing everything but don't care enough to get their hands dirty and do something to fix the problem. Recent years have revealed many cowards who will not stand up to defend the bride of Christ and instead just walk away. We don't need more cynics. (Cynics are about as useful as a Slinky on the moon.) What the church needs is not more whiny spectators but men and women committed to following Jesus at whatever the cost. Look at Jesus' responses to those who say they want to follow Him:

> As they were walking along the road, a man said to him, "I will follow you wherever you go."
>
> Jesus replied, "Foxes have holes and birds of the air have nests, but the Son of Man has no place to lay his head."
>
> He said to another man, "Follow me."
>
> But the man replied, "Lord, first let me go and bury my father."
>
> Jesus said to him, "Let the dead bury their own dead, but you go and proclaim the kingdom of God."

> Still another said, "I will follow you, Lord; but first let me go back and say good-by to my family."
>
> Jesus replied, "No one who puts his hand to the plow and looks back is fit for service in the kingdom of God." (Luke 9:57–62)

These three men all seem sincere. They are probably all good guys who want to be a part of what Jesus is doing. They probably want to make a difference, to serve, and to follow Jesus, but all three men have the same problem. They're all willing to be involved in Jesus' ministry, but none of them is truly willing to pay the price of commitment. The cost of following Jesus is high, and often we try to negotiate terms to get a better price as if Jesus is a used car dealer who needs to get us salvation before we leave the lot. Jesus is not a salesman! He is a Savior! Each of these men had something to which they were more committed than Christ. Jesus tells us exactly what it means to follow Him. He doesn't just want our belief. He is not looking for fans. Jesus is seeking our commitment to both Him and His church.

Jesus is not a salesman! He is a Savior!

I had a couple tell me they wanted to be missionaries. They did not go to church, didn't even really want to go to church. They called themselves Christians, but that was it. Basically, they wanted to be missionaries, not to take the message of Jesus to lost people across the world but so the church would fund their travel to exotic locations. I was blown away. They wanted funding, but they didn't want to commit to doing anything for Christ.

The problem that we are facing in the church today is that we have so many Christians who have made a decision to believe in Jesus but not a commitment to follow Him. We have people who are planning to, meaning to, trying to, wanting to, going to, we just don't have people who are doing it.

Involved ≠ committed. The difference between involvement and commitment is like the difference between eggs and ham at breakfast—the chicken was involved, but the pig was committed. What we have in our immediate society is not a culture of dedicated soldiers willing to storm the gates of hell, but a group of involved Christians who want to share in the victory without being a part of the labor. The involved Christian reserves the right to tell God no, because involvement does not require surrender. Commitment does. To commit is to bind yourself to something. It is a pledge or promise to *do* regardless of obstacles. How can we be committed to the church when we don't invest in its community? Some have even gotten to the point where they want to connect themselves with Christ's name and yet refuse to associate with His bride. They want Jesus without the church. If I had a close friend who wanted to spend time with me but not with my wife, that person would eventually stop getting my attention. When you are married, you are no longer single (profound, I know). It's a package deal. Jesus calls the church His bride. When we get Him, like it or not, the church is part of the package.

We have people who are planning to, meaning to, trying to, wanting to, going to, we just don't have people who are doing it.

The church is a vital part of our connection to Jesus. We should not give up on it because it is not perfect. Hebrews 10:25 instructs us to "not give up meeting together, as some are in the habit of doing." Most of us understand that to mean that we are to go to church. And so we do. Once a week. Maybe twice. We put in our time. But is that really participation in the fellowship of the community of the church? The early church gathered together daily. For them, meeting once a week would have seemed like forsaking the fellowship. We have a million excuses for why we can't commit further. You can attend church all your life without really committing to it. Being a part of a church family is about more than just showing up; it's about getting plugged in. Our actions betray the reality of our hearts.

The Hope of the Church: Community

Church attendance is not about numbers, and it is not about money. It is about connecting to the community of God. Matt Proctor, the president of Ozark Christian College, gave a chapel sermon where he talked about a friend of his who was a bit of a compulsive cleaner. When her nieces and nephews came over, she would take out a box of Legos for them to play with. Of course, when you give children a box of Legos, the first thing they are going to do is turn it upside down and dump all the Legos out. When this inevitably happened, his friend frantically put all the Legos back in the box. "No, no, no. I meant you can play with them *one at a time*." That is a problem, because you can't play with Legos one at a time. Legos were meant to be connected, and (like Legos) we are meant to be connected.[5]

Some people try to justify themselves with remarks like, "I can build a relationship with God without going to church," or "You don't have to go to church to be a Christian." My wife actually felt this way when I first met her. She had a personal prayer life and relationship with God and didn't really see a need to go to church. This had been her practice for years. The problem, however, was not that she didn't need church but that she didn't understand how important the role of the church was in her relationship with God. She didn't feel a need for church her whole life because she had never been to one that was alive. Once she experienced real relationships with real Christians, you couldn't keep her away with a SWAT team. To try to have Jesus without the church is like being married without ever living together. It's possible (perhaps), but not productive. It would be a marriage in name only, not marriage the way it was intended with all of its benefits (and hardships) and fullness and richness.

To try to have Jesus without the church is like being married without ever living together.

When we fail to be a part of the church, we are disobeying God. Understanding this rule is helpful, but only in showing us what we *should* do. Rules do not teach us how or why, only what. So when you are looking for what to do (or not do), the law is a great guide. We *should* invest ourselves in the church. The reason we should do it, however, is not found in the law but in love. The law teaches us right action; love teaches us proper motivation.

We get involved in the community of the church because we love God, and as such, we love the things that He loves.

I have known people who say, "I have a real problem with organized religion." Who doesn't? I am a pastor, and I dislike a religion. I want a relationship. A majority of Americans consider themselves Christian and yet their (supposed) belief doesn't change the way they live. This title, carried by the church for thousands of years, is being defiled because we have failed to live up to its meaning. The term *Christian* has become ambiguous. Maybe, in order to follow Christ, we have to stop being "Christian." OK, so I'm not willing to let go of "Christian," but we need to redeem the name by following Christ to the best of our ability and so become true Christians once again.

The church is the bride of Christ and the theater where God chooses to manifest His awesome glory. We must realize that the fullness of the Spirit of God does not dwell with each of us as individuals. God's Spirit only rests on us fully when we are together. The church is the body. The eye needs the hand as much as the hand needs the eye. We are complete only when we are together. In the community of the church, we have greater access to God's presence, His Spirit, His love, and His power.

It is not that these things are absent from our individual lives; it is that they are not reaching their full potential. My wife and I recently got our first laptop (only about ten years after they came out—we are really trendy). One of the things I noticed is that when the laptop is plugged into the wall with the charger, it seems to run a little faster. The laptop is designed to be portable. It has a battery that will last for several hours so when it gets unplugged, it does not shut down. If the laptop remains unplugged too long, the battery dies, and the computer has no life left. It will not work until the battery has been properly charged by being reconnected to the power source for a while.

Our spiritual lives are like that. We don't have to be plugged in to work. We even have access to all the same things unplugged, at least for a time. The problem is we can't stay unplugged for too long or we run out of energy and shut down. The church is our connection to the energy source. It enables us to run faster, brighter, and longer while at the same time charging our batteries. We need and should rightly long for opportunities to be a part of the church, as without it we will not last very long.

In Acts 2:42–47 we see a beautiful picture of the early church. You know what makes that picture so beautiful? Commitment. The church devoted themselves to the Word of God, communion, prayer, and fellowship.[6] The definition of the word for *devoted* used in Acts means to continue to do something with an intense effort despite possible difficulties.[7] That dedication established the foundation for a powerful and exciting church that helped grow the kingdom.

The church is devoted to community. Notice that this text says "all the believers" (v. 44). Most churches are lucky to have 20 percent this committed. That is a far cry from *all the believers*. We are lacking in that holistic investment in our churches today. In fact, what we have is hardly even involvement. Jesus says anyone who puts his hand to the plow and looks back is not fit for service in the kingdom of God (Luke 9:62). How many people in our churches fall into this category? Do you fall into this category?

This was a church with a proper set of priorities. Their focus was firstly on God and the kingdom through their personal connection to the church, and everything else came later. If God is the most important thing in your life, then the church is right there with Him as your top priority. This doesn't mean neglecting your family to be at the church every day. It means that just like your family, your relationship with the community of the church requires a regular investment of your time. If we can't make time for the church, are we really making time for God? If we can't make time for God, how can we ever really love our families?

We sometimes forget that while Jesus is our Savior, He is also our Lord. We don't like to think of Him as a God who disciplines because "my God is not like that." We prefer to think that He is in the business of saving, not of judging, not of condemning, not of ruling. As American theologian H. Richard Niebuhr says, what we have then is "a God without wrath [who] brought men without sin into a kingdom without judgment through the ministrations of a Christ without a cross."[8]

Rather than spending more time harping on how this is wrong, let's look at it from another angle. God is doing some amazing things in the world. Bible translations are being made available in new languages every year,[9] the underground church in China numbers in the tens of millions and is growing,[10] the Word is spreading, people are coming to a relationship with Jesus. Christian movies are being made and passion films taken to some of the remotest places on earth. Missions are on the rise. The kingdom is growing worldwide. If all these incredible things are being accomplished in the world with the few workers we have, what do you think God could do if the rest of us joined in? What would it look like if Christians all around the United States, or why not all around the world, dedicated themselves to the kingdom of God? Don't you see what we could do for the kingdom of God? If we would just open up our lives to Jesus, making His service our top priority, we could show the world what Jesus looks like.

There is a time for restraint, and there is a time to let loose the full passion of our heart; the time for restraint is over. It's time to stand up, step out, and change the world. No more holding on. No more holding back. It's time to go.

As it stands, churches have a hard time finding people to take care of their immediate needs. Let's change that. If you are reading this book, then I am talking to you: get involved. Get plugged in at your church. Find a way to invest yourself. Let's change the church's problem from "Where do we find the help we need?" to "What do we do with all the help we have?" The revolution begins now, and it starts with you.

Chapter Five

THE UNDEAD HEART

One of the weirder zombie movies I have seen was a Western called *Undead Alive.*[1] Elmer and Luke are two misfits who rob a corrupt local sheriff, unaware that a plague of zombies is sweeping the country. In this movie, zombies—while being undead and needing to eat the living—maintain the personality they had in life. Elmer and Luke befriend an Indian guide woman who helps them fight off the zombies until Elmer gets infected and in turn infects Luke.

The two now-zombie friends come to realize that the zombie condition is a result of an ancient Indian curse, and the only cure is to eat the heart of one of the Indians from the tribe who cursed them. So they kill their Indian guide friend, eat her heart, and are cured. They really got to the "heart" of the problem you might say. (I know, that was bad.)

One of the primary factors in creating Zombie churches is the heart. When the heart is neglected, it can easily become infected and cause the entire body to suffer.

Devious

It was no secret that Jesus and the religious leaders of His time did not get along. They viewed Jesus as a threat and wanted to put an end to His teaching. The trouble was, Jesus was a very popular teacher. If the religious leaders opposed Him directly, they would lose their popularity with the people and jeopardize their own power. So they took a more devious approach. They would send spies into crowds where Jesus was teaching to ask Him trick questions in hopes of getting Jesus to answer something incorrectly so they could discredit His teaching and get rid of Him. In Matthew 22:36–40 we see one such encounter with an expert in Mosaic Law who asked Jesus which is the most important commandment in the Law. The Jews had hundreds of laws in the Old Testament, not to mention the thousands of oral traditions they were expected to follow, so it could certainly prove difficult to select the undisputed greatest law. Jesus replies:

> "Love the Lord your God with all your heart and with all your soul and with all your mind." This is the first and greatest commandment. And the second is like it: "Love your neighbor as yourself." All the Law and the Prophets hang on these two commandments.

Jesus takes His answer from Deuteronomy 6:4, the Shema or Sh'ma, considered by the Jews to be the greatest commandment in the Law. Then Jesus mentions another commandment that is found in Leviticus 19. This passage is essential in our understanding of how we can love God. What does it mean to show God love? Love people. Sometimes we try to display our love for God by carrying out religious activities; we follow rituals, go to church, read the Bible. Are these really the things we do to show God we love Him? Isn't it possible to do these things without a love for God in

People who love God will read the Bible, but not everyone who reads the Bible loves God.

our hearts? There are plenty of atheists well-versed in Scripture who hate God. People who love God will read the Bible, but not everyone who reads the Bible loves God. Works don't require love.

So if we are to truly love God, it has to come from the core of who we are. If we love God with all of our heart, soul, and mind, what is left? Nothing of lasting significance. Take these away and you're left with a lifeless shell. Jesus is saying that we must love God with everything that we are.

Heart, Soul, Mind

"Love the Lord your God with all your *heart* and with all your soul and with all your mind . . ." (Matt. 22:37).

The heart is a vital organ. Life depends on it. In Revelation 2 Jesus speaks to the church in Ephesus and He commends them for their good deeds. He praises them for their dedication and commitment. Then He critiques them because they have lost their "first love." The Ephesians were holding their ground and they were doing the right things, but their hearts weren't in it. Their passion, their joy, the way in which they expressed their love for God had been lost, and Jesus tells them they need to get it back. They need to repent because a church without heart is a church without life.

If the heart goes bad, the whole body is in danger. A few years ago, while traveling in Italy, I explored the Vatican and St. Peter's Basilica. In visiting these "holy sites," one thing in particular caught my attention. Amidst all the beauty and splendor of thousands of years of history, these places were really just museums full of relics from the past. There was no life there—just glorified monuments of a time when life reigned. Missionaries to Italy and the rest of Europe find ministry extremely difficult because of the post-Christian culture there. Essentially these are countries where everyone knows who Jesus is and what He has done, but they don't much care. Christianity is little more than hollow religious activity in the name of God.

Many Italians don't seem to respond to the message of Jesus because they think they already have Him. They have been told for centuries that the life Jesus offers is in keeping the traditions and rituals of the church faithfully. So they go to mass several times a year, they make their annual confession, and they carry their prayer beads and all the while they walk around Jesus instead of walking with Jesus. Their heart has been lost. With it their passion, concern, and love for the things of God has gone as well. Life can't exist without the heart. If we are not careful, that may become our experience as well.

When we first come to Jesus, it is exciting. Our hearts are stirred with a wild flame of passion. As time goes on the flame flickers. If we do not continue to tend to our hearts by investing in our relationship with Jesus, then the flame dies down. We have seen this in the church: people who come because that is what they are supposed to do. People who treat the building as if it were holy and change their behavior when they are inside it, but outside the church . . . There is no heart to be found in mindlessly following rituals and regulations that don't mean anything to us. Faith without heart is what scares people away from organized religion.

Faith without heart is what scares people away from organized religion.

Sometimes the issue is not that we don't care but that we don't care about the things God cares about. Scripture refers to this as having a "hard heart." A hard heart is resistant to God while a heart of integrity leads us to a closer relationship with God. The heart is the area of our life in which God's influence manifests into faith; it's the principle point of our contact with God. Your heart reflects what you really believe. Jesus doesn't look to our appearance; He looks to the reality of our condition, which He finds in our hearts.

A healthy heart beats with the love of Jesus. The Christian heart is concerned with the things of God above all else. A person who has a healthy heart cares about what God cares about and seeks a genuine and intimate relationship with God like a bride seeks a relationship with her groom. When we love another person, we naturally seek to know that person. Love builds a passion inside of us that drives us toward intimacy.

Love creates not just a desire to know someone but also to be known by them. There is no devotion too great, no amount of time too long, for love essentially creates an unending desire to be with the one you love. We are created in the image of God and made both to love and to be loved by God. It is impossible for us to live a fully satisfying life without these two needs being met. When a Christian is without either of these two things, there should be a wild longing or passionate desire to obtain them.

Growing up, I had a friend named Andrew. When he came to Christ, it was like someone had poured gasoline all over a huge pile of logs and then lit it with a flame thrower. He was passionate and zealous for God.

He made a lot of people in the church uncomfortable. Andrew didn't play by other people's social rules. All he wanted to do was to love people and tell people about Jesus. So when people would talk about friends who didn't know Jesus, Andrew's answer was simple: go tell them.

Andrew's mom was his best friend in the world. One summer he was away at a church camp, hours from home, when his mom had an asthma attack in her sleep and died. It took two days to get ahold of him. When the youth minister he was with told him what had happened and explained that they'd made arrangements to fly him back home early so he could be with his family, Andrew's response, his instinctive reaction after hearing his mother was dead, was to say, "God must want me to minister to someone on the plane ride back."

Andrew had a passionate heart for God that could not be ignored. He would not be distracted. The central desire of Andrew's heart was to love God, and nothing was going to change that.

Hungry or Hateful

A healthy heart is reflected in the life of a Christian who has a genuine hunger and thirst for righteousness (Matt. 5:6). Think of some of the Psalms, a heart that loves God is a heart that relishes every moment spent with Him (Pss. 27:8; 38:8–10; 84:2). A healthy heart belongs to one who yearns for God like a lover. Every breath, every moment, every thought is consumed by devotion—obsession even—with God. This is a heart that could spend all day with God, and when it was time for bed, struggle to stay awake just to get a few more moments.

Understanding how to love God is not easy. Jesus gives us some help in John 14:15 where He says: "If you love me, you will obey what I command." So a part of loving God comes from obedience to the commands He gives us, the most important of which is to love. When we love God, we naturally love the things of God. To make it practical, Jesus likens it to how we judge a tree by its fruit (Matt. 7:15–23). Paul shows us what Christian fruit looks like:

> But the fruit of the Spirit is love, joy, peace, patience, kindness, goodness, faithfulness, gentleness and self-control. Against such things there is no law. Those who belong to Christ Jesus have crucified the sinful nature with its passions and desires. Since we live by the Spirit, let us keep in step with the Spirit. (Gal. 5:22–25)

The more our heart connects with the heart of God, the more these characteristics will be evident in our lives. These virtuous qualities are aspects of what it looks like to have the heart of God, but they still fail to capture the full essence.

As John points out in 1 John 4:20, if we do not love the people we can see, how can we love God whom we cannot see? Loving people is perhaps the best way in which we can express our love for God. When we love God and when we love others, we begin to mold our hearts and make them a bit more like the heart of God. To love God means we keep His commands, and God has commanded us to love Him and to love others. While we need God's unconditional love in order to truly offer love to others, the inverse is equally true.

God loves us all equally but not the same.

When we talk about God's love being unconditional, it is important to note how this works: God loves us all equally but not the same. All are sinners—whether lost or saved; all need God's love. Yet God loves each person according to the way that person needs His love. Just as parents with several children will (or ideally should) have the same amount of love for each child, that doesn't mean they love them all in the same way. Likewise, just because God's love is unconditional does not mean that everyone will be treated the same. Consider Jacob and Esau: the Bible says God loved Jacob but hated Esau (Mal. 1:2–3). What does that mean? We think of hate like a revolting, disgusting emotional feeling toward someone or something. Yet in a biblical sense, hate can also mean "to love less than." In the case of Jacob and Esau, God does not hate, despise, or loathe Esau (in spite of Esau's bad character); rather, He is saying that Jacob (despite his own character flaws) has been chosen to be a part of the line of Jesus the Messiah and not Esau. The issue is always relationship with God. This isn't talking about how God feels about individual people but makes the point that He doesn't love us all the same. We see the same thing in Luke 14:26 where Jesus says, "If anyone comes to me and does not *hate* his father and mother, his wife and children, his brothers and sisters—yes, even his own life—he cannot be my disciple." Jesus is not commanding us to literally hate our parents and family—to loathe or despise them. He is saying you have to love them less than Me. I have to be the priority. I have to be the focus. To hate can mean to make a lower priority than something or someone else.

Understanding how God loves us helps us love others. And that's why we need God's unconditional love to truly love people. But we also need to love people in order to love God. If you don't love others, then you don't love God. Does that sound harsh? Those who don't love are zombies walking around in darkness. It's biblical: "Whoever hates his brother is in the darkness and walks around in the darkness; he does not know where he is going, because the darkness has blinded him" (1 John 2:11).

We have a guy at the church who is a huge help around the building, getting projects done and fixing things that had been broken for a long time. In labor alone he probably saved the church at least ten thousand dollars (which for us was four to six weeks' total offering) during his first six months of attendance. One day I just wanted to say thank you for his work, and he looked at me like it was a waste of breath. He said that his service was the best way for him to spend time with God.

He was a great servant right from the day he walked in the doors, but God was still working on his heart. He had a challenging job, which required him to deal with some very difficult people. Every day he saw the broken and hurting people of the world. He witnessed firsthand the things hurting people do to each other while attempting to find what they are missing themselves. He saw pain, suffering, abuse. For a while this affected his attitude. He didn't have much patience for people and didn't really want to care about them. But within just a few months, God really started to shape Michael's heart.

As he grew closer to Jesus, Michael was transformed. When someone from the church was in the hospital for any reason, Michael was often the first person to arrive. I called him a few times on my way to the hospital, and somehow he would manage to arrive before I did. He told me one day as we were leaving the hospital that he didn't know what was happening to him, but for some reason he couldn't help loving people. He may not have known, but I did. Michael was experiencing the love of God, and it was overflowing from his life. When we love God with our whole heart, then God actually starts changing our heart for others.

Over the years (centuries actually), the church has really misrepresented Jesus.

It's a circle. Loving others does not come naturally to us, but when we love God, He enables us to love people. And then, as we love other people, we demonstrate our love for God.

In many Christians, the heart has become corrupted and has begun to decay. What once was passionate devotion has been replaced with dying embers, the eroding effects of an emotional disconnect from God. I don't think we ever intend for this to happen.

Over the years (centuries actually), the church has really misrepresented Jesus. We have judged and abused people for their lifestyles rather than loving them. Instead of care and compassion, we have offered disdain and disgust. It shouldn't matter what people have done or how they have lived. Even if someone is a porn star or a vehement atheist, there is no excuse for us to treat a person with anything less than the unconditional love of God. Our expressions of love may open the person's heart; it may not. One thing is certain: if the porn star and atheist don't see Jesus in us, they aren't going to accept Him anywhere else. We are to love them and to treat them as valuable, not as scum, because Jesus loves them and values them just as much as He does anyone else.

This is the beauty of the love of Jesus. He loves the crack dealer and the prostitute just as much as He loves the minister and the missionary. He views them as precious children.

We tend to view people we don't like as unloving people. We turn them into villains in our minds and blame them for a lot of our troubles. A good portion of the problems we face are not because people are evil but because we are imperfect, hurting people who, in efforts to protect ourselves, sometimes hurt others.

The movie *Hotel Rwanda* is based on real events portraying one of the worst atrocities in human history. In the country of Rwanda, in a three-month period, as many as a million people were brutally murdered. A man named Paul Rusesabagina (played by Don Cheadle) saved over a thousand refugees by housing them at a hotel he managed. While they are at the hotel, cameraman Jack Daglish (Joaquin Phoenix) manages to get some footage of the genocide occurring all around them.

> PAUL: "I am glad you got that footage and that the world will see it. It is the only way people might intervene."
>
> JACK: "Is it good to show if no one intervenes?"
>
> PAUL: "How can they not intervene when they witness such atrocities?"
>
> JACK: "I think if people see this footage, they will say 'oh, that's horrible,' and then go on eating their dinners."

Where is our heart? How can seeing the suffering of others not prompt us to do something about it? What kind of hatred prevents us from responding to another's need?

Apathetic

One of the great dangers facing the church today and also a primary factor in creating Zombie churches is the rising tide of apathy. We are aware of the needs of the world. We know there are children dying because they can't get medicine for curable diseases. We know there are people starving who eat less in a week than we throw away after a single meal. We know there are children being sold into slavery to be used for perverse pleasures. We know there are terrible acts being committed all across the world, and yet we generally do nothing.

Apathy has stained our lives so pervasively that we don't even recognize it anymore. We know of all the needs in the world, and we know there are many needs in our communities and our own backyards, and yet that knowledge hasn't led us to do anything about it. We talk about it, we just don't act. Our inaction reveals the true apathy of our hearts. I understand the feeling of powerlessness that comes from realizing the needs of the world. When there are millions of people starving, what can one person really do to help?

Overcoming powerlessness starts with realizing that my role is to be available, not to save the world. We will not solve world hunger, sex trafficking, or any other issue. The church is God's redemptive agent in the world; yet it is still God who does the redeeming.

There is only one reason we don't feed the hungry, tend to the sick and abused, and help our fellow man. . . . To put it bluntly: we don't care.

When we are available to God, we can be tools God uses to help reduce these problems. In making yourself available, perhaps you will take a short-term missions trip. Perhaps you will spend much time in prayer, where you honestly pour your heart out to God. Perhaps you are able to use your unique gifts to do something about a particular problem. However it looks, it will require caring enough to do *something.*

There is only one reason we don't feed the hungry, tend to the sick and abused, and help our fellow man. It is not ignorance. To put it bluntly: we don't care. The modus operandi of our American culture is to only care about what directly affects our lives. If it doesn't interfere with you and your own personal sphere, the tendency is to not care at all.

We are not the first people to wrestle with this problem. Look at Israel:

> This is what the LORD Almighty says: "These people say, 'The time has not yet come for the LORD's house to be built.'"
>
> Then the word of the LORD came through the prophet Haggai: "Is it a time for you yourselves to be living in your paneled houses, while this house remains a ruin?"
>
> Now this is what the LORD Almighty says: "Give careful thought to your ways. You have planted much, but have harvested little. You eat, but never have enough. You drink, but never have your fill. You put on clothes, but are not warm. You earn wages, only to put them in a purse with holes in it."
>
> This is what the LORD Almighty says: "Give careful thought to your ways. Go up into the mountains and bring down timber and build the house, so that I may take pleasure in it and be honored," says the LORD. "You expected much, but see, it turned out to be little. What you brought home, I blew away. Why?" declares the LORD Almighty. "Because of my house, which remains a ruin, while each of you is busy with his own house. Therefore, because of you the heavens have withheld their dew and the earth its crops. I called for a drought on the fields and the mountains, on the grain, the new wine, the oil and whatever the ground produces, on men and cattle, and on the labor of your hands." (Hag. 1:2–11)

Haggai was one of the few prophets to see positive results among the people of God, showing us what can happen when we listen to the Word of God and work according to what He has said. We see the problem right away. The people had their priorities in the wrong place. They had become tolerant, even apathetic about the rebuilding of the temple. One of the primary ways apathy is seen is when God's work is being neglected by His people.

In 586 B.C. the Babylonian king Nebuchadnezzar invaded and conquered Jerusalem. The city was razed and the temple destroyed. The Israelites were taken into Babylon as captives where they would remain for seventy years. In 536 B.C. the Babylonian Empire fell to the Persians. Later, the Persian king Cyrus gave the Jews permission to return to Jerusalem with the explicit purpose of rebuilding the temple of the Lord. So a man named Zerubbabel led fifty thousand people back to Jerusalem. This was a dream come true. After seventy years of captivity, the Jews were finally able to go home.

What a great joy this would have been. They started rebuilding the temple. They cleared away the rubble and even laid the foundation before problems arose and the people stopped working. At the first sign of opposition, the people of Israel gave up. They did not stop rebuilding their own lives. They just stopped working on the temple. So every time they went to the temple for sacrifices or for worship, they would look around and know that this wasn't right. Yet they just didn't care enough to do the work to finish it. So for fourteen years the rebuilding of the temple of the Lord was neglected. The people were apathetic and needed an awakening. So God sent Haggai to wake them up.

From the look of churches in America today, I think we're in need of the same wake-up call. The process apathy takes in our lives is subtle but dangerous. We get out of the habit of attending church services. We get out of the habit of praying, of worshipping, of serving, of studying the Word, and it doesn't really bother us that much. We feel a bit guilty at first but not enough to do anything about it. Before we know it, our spiritual lives revolve around little more than sporadic church attendance and a few prayers said before meals. Our concern for the salvation of others dwindles as we become apathetic about anything that doesn't interfere with our free time.

A few years ago a well-known Christian speaker came to preach at the college I was attending. While talking about the heart of God for the lost and our role in the process, he said, "Ten thousand people die and go to hell every day and Christians just don't give a [*censored expletive*]." (He actually said the word, but you can get the point without my typing it.) The speaker waited a moment and continued: "You know what the sad part about that is? You care more about the fact that I just said [*repeat of previously used, still censored expletive*] than about the fact that ten thousand people die every day and go to hell." His point was dead-on. We care so much for the laws that we lose sight of the people. A roomful of ministers-in-training were caught up more by their feelings about his graphic word choice than about the overall inaction of the church to reach out to the lost people of the world. Our hearts were in the wrong place. We knew the stats and just didn't care enough.

There is a sociological condition proposed by Paul Lazarsfeld called narcotizing dysfunction.[2] The idea is that the more we become informed, the less active we become. We mistake knowing about something and even discussing it as actually doing something about it. We become concerned, informed, and inactive. We allow our knowledge of the problem to justify our unwillingness to do something about it, and rather than taking steps to make a difference, we exchange meaningless words with the choir on how the problem could be solved, when our own action might have prevented it from becoming a problem in the first place.

The sad truth is, if we as Christians spent as much time evangelizing as we did talking about evangelism, then the gospel would have impacted a great number of people that it has not yet reached. If we spent as much time reading the Bible as we did talking about the little pieces we know, we would know it and possibly do what it says much better. Truthfully, if we spent as much time praying and working for the repentance of sinners as we did for the comforts of saints, then perhaps the world would be saved already. We tell ourselves we care about those in need. We talk about how terrible it is for them. We are all keenly aware of the commission God has given us. We all know we have a responsibility to take the gospel to the world. Yet rather than doing something about it, we make excuses to justify our inactivity in the global mission of God.

When you rip God's heart . . . out of a church, then you're left with a Zombie church.

Apathy can completely immobilize us. When you rip God's heart—which desperately yearns for lost and hurting people—out of a church, then you're left with a Zombie church. Apathy robs us of joy and meaning by stealing purpose away from us. Apathy destroys creativity, stunts growth, drains energy, and leaves us with an overall feeling of depression. We are trapped in some plane in between life and death, living without really living and dying before we are actually dead.

Put aside all the excuses. Let's face it: we don't care because we don't really want to care. But consider this: When we sit and do nothing, we are withholding life from a dying world. What could be more hateful than that? We need to do more than just talk. We need to do more than just exchange theories and ideas; we need to go out into the world and offer them the life that we have.

The problem is the Great Commission does not state, "Go make disciples of the world, baptizing them in the name of the Father and the Son and the Holy Spirit and teaching them to obey unless it is hard, unless you have better things to do, unless you are busy, unless you don't know what to say . . ." No, God says go. Make disciples, baptize them in My name, and teach them to obey everything I have commanded you. And our excuses do not justify our disobedience.

The Wrong Battles

The church fights the wrong battles. (All those people who have felt judged or condemned by the church understand exactly what I'm talking about.) It spends too much time dealing with what is seen and not enough time dealing with the condition of the heart, like a doctor who prescribes Advil for a brain tumor. It may mask one of the symptoms, but it doesn't cure the problem. Too quick to judge, too slow to love, we evaluate people based on their appearance or their attitude. *Don't use foul language. Don't go to bars. Don't have premarital sex.* These instructions are not antibiblical, but they come across as self-righteous and hypocritical (especially when people see us doing the very things we say not to do). People's broken hearts need healing, not cosmetic surgery.

Life in the church is not about setting up the right rules. It is about connecting people with Jesus. It is time the church stopped dealing with the outside and started looking at the heart. We should never have to talk with someone who uses vulgar language about their language. What we should do is connect that person to Jesus by "being Jesus" in his or her life. As we die to ourselves and are raised up to new life in Christ, Christ lives in us, and we are His hands and feet. So we love people, pray for them, encourage them, and support them. It is not our job to prevent them from sinning but simply to bring them to Jesus. The church needs to stop fighting the symptoms and the people who have them, and start dealing with the real problem: a lack of connection to life.

Never Lose Heart

Internationally known evangelist Reinhard Bonnke says, "Jesus will rescue you from the pit, but He will not rescue you from the La-Z-Boy."

Jesus stands at the door and knocks. He will not force you out of your slumps. He will not throw you into action. He knocks. It's up to you to answer. Make no mistake; our inaction betrays our unbelief. Haggai addressed this problem of apathy, and the people of Israel changed. We do not have to live meaningless lives; God has given us a purpose. He has given us a mission: to take the good news of the life that He offers to the world. In Matthew 25:34–46 God shares with us His heart for those in need. If we will hear His words and turn back to Him, we can overcome this apathy. God also makes this promise to His people in the Old Testament, in 2 Chronicles:

> If my people, who are called by my name, will humble themselves and pray and seek my face and turn from their wicked ways, then will I hear from heaven and will forgive their sin and will heal their land. (2 Chron. 7:14)

Even prior to Jesus' redemptive work on the cross, the heart of God to heal, to forgive, and to rescue His people from the grips of apathy and sin is evident. If God was faithful to such a promise before Jesus' arrival, how much more then can we trust in this promise as we are covered by the blood of His precious Son?

We cannot sit back any longer and watch as our churches are conditioned to seek safety, then comfort, which becomes complacency, which quickly turns to apathy. Finding a church with a healthy heart is already difficult. We cannot watch the infection spread from church to church and do nothing.

There is a simple cure, though: do *something.*

Our Cornerstone church family started doing an event called White Saturday, which took place on the Saturday after Thanksgiving. Families from the church got together to make cookies and deliver them to all the houses in the neighborhoods surrounding our church. We included a note from the church saying we just wanted to show them the love of Jesus in a practical way. We also included a few "tickets" and told them that if they had children, from infant to teenager, we had been taking gift donations for the last few months, and they could come pick out a gift for each child to help with the holiday season.

The church may have problems, but it is not beyond repair.

The church is located in a poor community, and we started doing this during a time of financial crisis. We realized a lot of families were going to be struggling through Christmas, and we wanted to help. It wasn't a hugely significant act, but it had a significant effect on the community. Four months later, I was still hearing people talk about how much this meant to them.

You see, there is hope. It starts with one. One step. One kind deed. One loving word. One. The church may have problems, but it is not beyond repair. All that is needed is for us to turn around and go in another direction. God can do incredible things with one single act of faithfulness. Taking that one step may be all that is needed to start a chain of events that brings life back to the church. You don't have to be a leader of the church to take that first step. Life comes from following after Jesus. You can be the spark that sets the church ablaze.

We need to bring the heart back into our relationship with Jesus.

One of my favorite scenes in *Braveheart* comes toward the end of the movie where Robert the Bruce is having a conversation with his father after he has betrayed William Wallace by fighting for the British. "I have nothing," Robert the Bruce says. "Men fight for me because if they do not, I throw them off my land and I starve their wives and children. Those men who bled the ground red at Falkirk fought for William Wallace. He fights for something that I never had. And I took it from him, when I betrayed him. I saw it in his face on the battlefield and it's tearing me apart."

His father responds, "All men betray. All lose heart."

After so long playing the politician and reluctant leader, Robert the Bruce finally steps up in a moment of passion and proclaims: "I don't want to lose heart! I want to believe as he does."

That's powerful. We can live in a perpetual state of numbness by slowly conditioning ourselves not to feel the void in our lives, or we can rage against this growing apathy and cry out for ourselves: "I don't want to lose heart!"

Chapter Six

LOST SOUL

In the 2008 *Day of the Dead*,[1] an influenza-like epidemic breaks out in a small Colorado town. The military is dispatched to quarantine the area. As it turns out, the infection is the result of some scientific experimentation that went wrong, resulting in an illness that turns people into flesh-eating zombies. A few survivors are forced to try to escape the area if they hope to live. One of them, Private Bud, gets bitten, as often happens in zombie movies. He tries to hide his condition as he slowly begins to transform.

The writers of this movie allowed for zombies to retain some aspects of their personality even as they became ravenous killers. Since Bud was a vegetarian in his pre-zombie existence, he retains this deeply held conviction in his zombie state. Apparently the vegetarian condition is more powerful than the ravenous desires of a flesh-eating zombie. So here we have Bud the vegetarian zombie: he knows who his friends are and even tries to help them by fighting other zombies. He cannot communicate or function the way he did when he was alive, but he has the same knowledge. Something about him—the deepest part of what makes him Bud, his *soul* if you will—has remained unchanged.

Heart, *Soul*, Mind

"Love the Lord your God with all your heart and with all your *soul* and with all your mind . . ." (Matt. 22:37).

The soul is perhaps the most mysterious part of who we are. In our scientific age the soul, or the spirit as we sometimes think of it, is intriguing because it cannot be reasonably measured or seen. As a result some treat the soul with an unhealthy fascination. Spiritualists and mystics neglect all the other aspects of a person in their overemphasis on the soul. On the other hand empiricists and rationalists will treat the soul as a vestigial part of the human body, hardly recognizing it exists at all. What did Jesus mean when He referred to the *soul*?

The soul is the part of a person or living thing that gives them life.

The Greek word for *soul* is *psychē*. *Pyschē* also means life. In the Septuagint (the Greek translation of the Old Testament) and the New Testament, *psychē* is used to refer to the principle of life itself.[2] The soul is the part of a person or living thing that gives them life. Our soul is the force that drives us either toward things of this world or toward the things of heaven. In Psalm 63:1 we see the yearning that exists in a soul that is focused on God:

> O God, you are my God
> earnestly, I seek you;
> my soul thirsts for you,
> my body longs for you,
> in a dry and weary land
> where there is no water.
> (Ps. 63:1)

Your soul is essentially . . . *you*. Your soul makes you who you are. The will or drive of your soul is what prevents you from acting on some things while allowing you to act on others.

Perhaps it is best to think of the soul as the source of our behavior. When we study the reasoning process and the interplay between emotions, reason, and will in a person's life, we call that psychology. Psychology is the study of human behavior. To this day when we study the behavior of a person, we connect it to their psyche, their soul.

Soulless

You know where I'm going here. So many churches in America have no soul (and I'm not talking about the mysterious force that gives power to gospel music in Southern Baptist churches). The soul is the life of the church—it's what makes the church . . . *church*. When the soul is missing in the church, then we have no purpose. The church does not exist to keep its doors open; it exists to seek and save the lost. The purpose of our existence is to glorify God by pointing people to Jesus. And we do that by standing up for truth, defending what is right, caring for the hurting . . . When did church become a building?

The purpose of our existence is to glorify God by pointing people to Jesus.

Pastors get caught up in the power and respect given to their office and forget that their ministry is not about themselves. It's like we get so focused on doing things for God that we forget to invite Him to be a part of the process. Leaders sometimes get so blinded by control that they begin acting in inappropriate ways to ensure they keep their positions. Churches get so focused on numerical success that they begin sacrificing the truth of the Word for popular opinion. Many churches and pastors spend more time worrying about what people will think than about what God thinks. Allowing others to influence our actions or to hinder us from doing what is right is referred to in Scripture as the "fear of man." Jesus says it's a bad idea.

We all come to the church for different reasons but there is one thing we should all get out of it: *life*. The life of a church is found in a real relationship with Jesus that is built on the foundation of the grace of God. Not rules. Not guilt trips. When the soul of a church disconnects from Jesus, it will no longer be able to offer life and it will begin to turn into a Zombie church.

The church has a responsibility to preach the truth of the Word of God without watering it down or catering to the audience. The soul, the essence of the church, has become so tainted by our consumer culture that we don't even see the problem with the way things are. Churches should not be run by popular opinion. Churches should not revamp the Word of God to keep from offending people.

I knew a pastor who was a very nice man. He had a good heart and he really loved people. He was so insecure with himself that he was constantly making enemies out of people from the church. He had absolute power in the church but was afraid to lead people where they needed to go. It was an unhealthy setup with no checks and balances and no one could challenge or discipline him. There was always a scapegoat upon whom he would blame the church's problems. Slowly but surely that church has withered away because it has had no direction, no vision, no motivation. It lost its soul. When the church starts putting other things above being like Jesus to the world, then its soul becomes tainted. This church wasn't fulfilling its purpose.

Many churches try to accomplish their purpose through programs and events, but what do they accomplish? How is the kingdom furthered by one more Christmas Eve service? How does that lost person down the street find Jesus through a church potluck?

Of course there is nothing wrong with having events that just get people together in fellowship, but there has to be something more. The church is not a social club; it is part of a kingdom. And while some things should be done "just for fun," we must also have a kingdom mind-set. The soul of the church must not lose sight of the purpose of its existence. A church with a healthy soul will move with a strange sense of direction that accents everything it does. Understanding that we exist to glorify God and to seek and save the lost

Would the community around you notice if the church stopped meeting?

gives our churches a purpose; our soul drives us to work toward achieving this goal.

A lot of churches in America could close their doors and the world would keep on spinning. Zombie churches. They could shut down without the community ever noticing. This is perhaps the best test to see if your church is living or undead. Would the community around you notice if the church stopped meeting? Would they feel a loss? If the only people who would notice a church closing are the people who go to it, then it is probable that the church is already undead or close to it.

To love God with all of your soul is to love Him with your will, your determination, your personality—your whole self. If that sounds abstract and confusing, that's because it is sort of abstract and confusing. To love God with your soul is to love God with what you do and with who you are.

Yada, Yada, Yada

Yada is a Hebrew word meaning "to know" or "to understand" and is used commonly in the Old Testament.[3] Related ideas are also expressed in the New Testament describing our relationship with God. Jesus says:

> I do not accept praise from men, but I know you. I know that you do not have the love of God in your hearts. (John 5:41–42)

Jesus knows us. *Yada* implies a personal knowledge. It is more than just knowing about something; it is true knowing. When Jesus knows us, He is not saying I know your height and your weight, and where you went to school, and where you work, and your favorite pizza topping. *Yada* is not knowing about superficial facts.

True knowledge "knowing" is bound up in a relationship with God. Proverbs 1:7 tells us "the fear of the Lord is the beginning of knowledge." Elsewhere in the Bible the intimacy of this knowledge is used to describe sexual intimacy within a marriage covenant. When Adam lay with Eve, it was said he "knew" her, they had *yada*; two becoming so intimately bonded that they are one (Gen. 4:1 ESV). What God desires to have with us is an intimacy where we are so bonded to Him that there is no separation between us: oneness with Him. *Yada.*

Sometimes people distinguish between head knowledge and what they call heart knowledge. The distinction tends to refer to the difference between a mental awareness of something and truly understanding it. *Yada* is about knowing what makes another person tick, makes her unique, what makes her who she is.

Yada is a knowing that understands the hurts and obstacles a person has faced in life. It is knowing his core motivations and aspirations in addition to the little things about him like his favorite pizza topping or ice cream flavor. *Yada* is seeing someone in the fullness of his humanity, knowing someone for who he is. Knowing in this sense is holistic.

Knowledge in the Old Testament implies knowledge that is personal, experiential, emotional, and relational. Thus knowledge is not based on intellectual comprehension as much as it is based on a personal relationship between two parties. To know is to invest in another person as if he is a mystery to be solved or a treasure to be found.[4]

Yada is knowing in truth.

> Now this is eternal life: that they may know you, the only true God, and Jesus Christ, whom you have sent. (John 17:3)

Eternal life is as simple as knowing God. Imagine the depth of this for a moment. The greatest thing we can do in this life is to know God. When we have experienced God's awesome power in our lives, that is only a fraction of who He is; eternal life is getting to fully know Him. Imagine being able to fully know God. God is the greatest treasure that exists. Eternal life is finding that treasure.

There are two levels at which we develop this knowledge of God. The first is through sensory experience. It comes from seeing and experiencing God's work in your life. This is the part that helps us know Him.

To know isn't to know *about,* it is to attempt to have *yada.* That is what God desires to have with us. The problem we face comes when knowledge gets in the way of understanding. A lot of people have accumulated an incredible amount of knowledge about God—they can quote Scriptures and recite facts very well—yet they do not have any real understanding. They do not really know God.

The problem is that sometimes we *yada yada yada* instead of having *yada*. If we are not careful, all the stuff we know about God can prevent us from actually knowing God. Knowledge by itself can be dangerous and can get in the way of what God is saying to us.

Some of the things we need to hear the most are things we already "know." But when we already know it, we often refuse to accept it as the solution to our problem. One of the most unreliable people I know would make promise after promise to do things. Each time, he would fail to follow through. I finally told him that he needed to stop making promises and just do what he said he was going to do. I reminded him of Matthew 5:33–37 and encouraged him to simply let his yes be yes and his no be no. "I know, I know, I know," he responded. He had heard this before, and he didn't want to listen. The very thing he needed to hear was something he couldn't hear because he already knew it. *Yada yada yada* gets in the way of *yada*.

***Yada yada yada* gets in the way of *yada*.**

God doesn't expect us to be a walking encyclopedia of biblical knowledge; He wants us to know Him, to be in relationship with Him. This means not only hearing but allowing our understanding of God to change the way we live. Like the wise builder who laid the foundation of his house on the rock, we learn to let our knowledge of God change us.

What God desires from us is what any husband or wife would desire from a spouse: to know and to be known in such a way that changes things. It is one thing for a husband to know that his wife loves it when he cleans her car. It is another thing entirely for him to use that knowledge. If the husband knows and yet does not act, how is that any different than if he didn't know? In fact it is worse because he knew what she liked and chose

Knowledge without action is worse than ignorance.

not to do it. Knowledge without action is worse than ignorance.

When I was a boy, I got into a lot of trouble. I was often tempted to lie to try to get out of trouble. One thing never ceased to amaze me. My mother always knew. If I tried to hide something, if I tried to deceive her, somehow she always knew. It wasn't because she was psychic; my mom knew when I was lying because she knew me. She knew me better than I knew myself, I think; so when I tried to hide the truth, she could see it all over my face. That's the difference really between knowing someone and knowing about them. You can Google any actress you want and learn all kinds of things about her, but that doesn't mean you are a part of her life. It doesn't mean you know her. To know requires a relationship, it requires spending time together.

What we see in our churches is a lot of knowing about God without a true understanding of who God really is. We have this tendency to try to make God like us instead of trying to make ourselves like God. Some view God as all love and no justice. Wrong. Others view God as all wrath but no love. Wrong again. Any time we want God to take sides—to be Republican or Democrat, to be Methodist or Christian Reformed—we make God small. I know some of you are blown away by that. God is also not a Catholic, or a Presbyterian, or a Baptist, or a Pentecostal, or any other subgroup that we have created in the church. Look at this passage from the book of Joshua:

> Now when Joshua was near Jericho, he looked up and saw a man standing in front of him with a drawn sword in his hand. Joshua went up to him and asked, "Are you for us or for our enemies?"
>
> "Neither," he replied, "but as commander of the army of the LORD I have now come." (Josh. 5:13–14)

Joshua asks the question we so often want to ask of God: "Are You with me or against me?" The angel's answer is simple: "Neither, I am with God." So often we seem to think that God is on our side. This is not how God works. God is not playing favorites and siding with us; He is giving us the opportunity to side with Him. God doesn't come to take sides, He comes to take over.

God doesn't come to take sides, He comes to take over.

It's time for the church to stop being afraid of itself because it is made of many parts and to start working together as a functional entity. I had a conversation a few years ago with a guy I knew. At the time we were both training for ministry at very different schools. We discussed our plans for the future and I told him that my dream was to see a church that was truly nondenominational, or perhaps interdenominational since nondenominational is its own denomination at this point. Where Baptists and Lutherans, Catholics and Protestants, Methodists and Pentecostals, Reformists and traditionalists, thinkers and feelers, conservatives and free thinkers, and any other denomination you could think of put their differences aside and unite under a common goal of sharing the love of Jesus with the world. In His ministry, Jesus consistently broke cultural, ethnic, gender, and social barriers, uniting people who had nothing else in common but Him. Perhaps it is time Jesus' church started looking like Jesus. As I flushed out my dream for the "ideal" church, his response was, "Never gonna happen." He said there would be no way to get people of different denominations to rally together into a functional team or body. All you would get, he said, was a bunch of people fighting amongst themselves. While I adamantly disagree with his conclusion, I have seen where he got it.

That is the trouble: we care too much about what the Bible says and not enough about what it means. We get too focused on the details of the law and not focused enough on the heart of the law. We have too many hardliners and dictators of the faith and not enough people who are seeking to share the heart of Jesus. The church often seems to care more about rules than it does about people; doctrine, not Jesus, sits on the throne of their worship. Christ followers seem to have a hard time getting along with anyone who does not completely agree with their view of God. Any variation

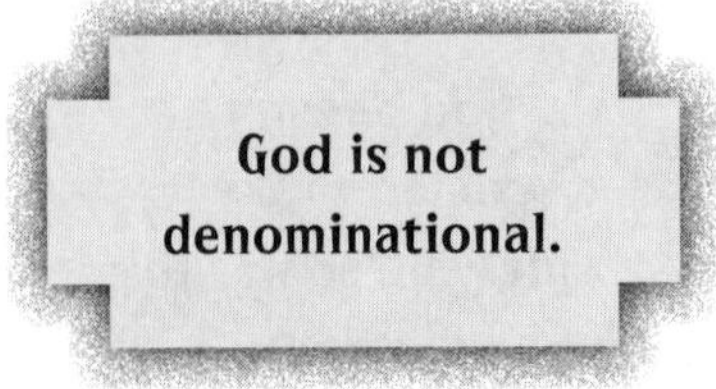

is considered "false teaching" or heresy, and the culprit treated as an enemy of the faith.

God is not denominational. These distinctions don't mean anything to Him. Churches spend time fighting and arguing over petty theological differences while the world falls apart and non-Christians die. Until we are willing to shed the non-salvational issues that separate us and learn to work together under the authority of the one true God, we can never really call ourselves a church that is alive. My first ministry was at a small church where there were Pentecostals and cessationists, Catholics, Baptists, and various others. Yet despite theological differences in some smaller dogmatic areas, these people could sit next to each other in love because they realized that we have more uniting us than we have dividing us. I have been blessed to be a part of a church that really doesn't care about denominations. All they want to do is love Jesus. That sentiment is rare in the church and it is beautiful.

Losing Focus

Denominations are not as harmless as we like to think. Our denominational separations in the church are in many ways like a corporate act of the eye saying to the hand I don't need you. We aren't helping the kingdom when we divide it into pieces. This process defiles the purity of Jesus' bride. We have no right to do that. There are some issues that are worth fighting over, but many of the divisions we bring into the church are not essential doctrines and do not relate to salvation. Take for example the Church of Christ and the Christian Church: two different denominations whose primary, if not exclusive, difference is the use of instruments in worship. There are certain teachings that every Christian must hold onto, but it seems that the teachings that most divide us are things that are not essential to salvation. Until the church learns how to let go of some of these petty theological differences and to focus on God, we can never be a church that is alive. As the bride of Christ we ought to value unity with other believers more than being right on every single nuance of biblical interpretation. That is not to say we shouldn't study or discuss those things, but some things are not worth dividing over. If I tried to become polygamous, my wife would rightly find that to be a divide-the-relationship issue; whereas if I tried to become a vegetarian, that really shouldn't matter (though knowing how much I like a good steak, she would be within her right to wonder about my sanity). Some things are not worth causing division over. In the book of Acts, when the Holy Spirit is active and involved in the church, you know what we see? The Holy Spirit works to create unity in the church, not division. So how do you think He feels about all the separations we have added to it?

It seems fitting that in several places Paul refers to Christians as soldiers. This is a very helpful image for understanding the problem that has developed in the church. Soldiers are trained to fight. What happens when you stick a bunch soldiers in a barracks and leave them with nothing to do for long periods of time? They fight. Take away their enemy and they will fight each other. Soldiers are dangerous when they have lost sight of their enemy or their purpose. It is important that we avoid the danger of distraction, because this really damages our soul.

We live in a culture that is entertaining itself to death . . .

We live in a culture that is entertaining itself to death: watch movies, listen to music, watch TV, play games, sit back and relax, read books, exercise, eat, drink, and be merry. Then there is the work side to busyness: mow the law, change the lightbulbs, write a proposal, decorate the house, take out the trash, water the plants, make a conference call, fix the sink, sign the contract. There are countless demands on our time. The danger here is that most of these things are not evil in and of themselves. So they do not send up any warnings. Yet, while we keep ourselves busy, we neglect the things that really matter.

Worry, stress, poverty, riches, trials, free time—all of these can be used by the enemy to keep your thoughts off God. The tools really don't mean anything to our enemy. All he cares about is the end. If he can use money to distract you, he will. If he can use a lack of money to distract you, he will. He will use anything available to him to stop you from growing in the vine. Jesus talks about this in the parable of the soils:

> A farmer went out to sow his seed. As he was scattering the seed, some fell along the path, and the birds came and ate it up. Some fell on rocky places, where it did not have much soil. It sprang up quickly, because the soil was shallow. But when the sun came up, the plants were scorched, and they withered because they had no root. Other seed fell among thorns, which grew up and choked the plants. Still other seed fell on good soil, where it produced a crop—a hundred, sixty or thirty times what was sown. (Matt. 13:3–8)

Do you see how many ways there are to keep the seeds from growing? The seed in this story is the message of God's Word, which springs to life and grows in the hearts of His children. We are the soil. Some of us are rocky and there is no place for God's Word to fit. Some of us have thorns and baggage from our life that keep us from growing. The good soil is the only soil that produces a fruitful crop, yet in contrast there are so many different ways to keep the seeds from growing into a crop. Toss some rocks on the soil, plant something else, put some thorns in. All of these things can accomplish the Devil's ultimate goal.

The truth is, the Devil's job is easy.

The truth is, the Devil's job is easy. He does not have to get you to become an axe murderer or serial rapist; all he has to do is to keep your mind off eternal things. To this end he employs some wonderful tactics. He keeps us focused on the ordinary. We spend so much time worrying about the errands we need to run and the day's checklist that we do not focus on important things. We must learn to change our mind-set.

When you go to the store for milk, you are not there to get milk. *I'm not?* The milk is not your primary agenda; it is the excuse you have to go out and to glorify God with your life. Make sure you get the milk or you may be in trouble when you return home, but the milk is a secondary objective. We need to transform our thinking. Every moment of every day is an opportunity for us to know God better and to show His love to the world. Your purpose is to show God's love to the people you come in contact with, whether a cashier at Wal-Mart, your bank teller, or better yet the very displeased lady who works for the government at the DMV and spends most of her day being yelled at by impatient or rude motorists. Your purpose is not to renew your license plates; it is to be the only friendly face that woman will see today! Every person is an opportunity.

Sometimes the hardest part is not in asking for forgiveness but in accepting the fact that Jesus offers it.

Glorifying God is not hard—simply showing His love is enough. It's easy for us to become distracted. Life is busy. But when we learn to see every moment as an opportunity, then instead of trying to find time for God, we make God a part of everything we do.

Our enemy uses the distractions of day-to-day life to keep us from investing in eternal things. Where this tactic may fail he has plenty of back-ups. He pushes our thoughts to the past and some of our mistakes. He gets our focus onto regrets or unfinished projects. The guilt alone will keep us from feeling that we have the right to think of heavenly things. Even when we know past choices have been forgiven, these feelings still overwhelm.

We have all made mistakes. Sometimes the hardest part is not in asking for forgiveness but in accepting the fact that Jesus offers it. When the echo of past mistakes reverberates in your ears, there is a simple way to disarm the enemy of our souls: use the sword power of God's Word. Maybe you've heard this one: "There is now no condemnation for those who are in Christ Jesus" (Rom. 8:1). If you are a believer in Jesus, forgiven and in Him, then there is:

No condemnation.

No guilt.

No shame.

Touché!

You are free!

Bottom line, while we are distracted or full of regret, we are neglecting the work that God has called us to do, which is to stay focused on Jesus.

Distracted

A close friend of mine was at a high school camp where they played a very interesting game. The game was called Angels and Demons. Most of the kids playing would be blindfolded. A few were selected to be angels and a few were selected to be demons. It was the job of the angels to lead the blindfolded campers to a cabin representing heaven. It was the job of the demons to keep them from heaven. There was a dumpster, representing hell, to which a demon could lead a camper to get the camper out of the game. The blindfolded campers could not remove their blindfolds until they reached either the cabin or the dumpster.

Without knowing who was a demon or who was an angel, the blindfolded campers had to decide which voices to trust. They had to rely on their ability to discern from the voices they heard. My friend was an angel in this game. He had been leading this one camper toward the cabin for a long time. He was walking with him, encouraging him, helping him with the journey. Then a camper who was playing a demon came up and began to lure the other camper away. As the camper was being lured, my friend said: "Wait, don't go. You have been listening to my voice this whole time. I have led you safely this far and we are almost there. Trust me. Follow me. You know my voice." The camper did. He followed him to the cabin and made it safely because he knew the voice and he trusted it.

The lesson this game teaches is so important. We need to recognize God's voice and the kinds of things He leads us to do, and we need to recognize our enemy's voice and the kinds of things he would entice us to do. How can we learn to distinguish between these two voices? You get to know the source. The better you know God, the more you will distinguish His voice from the rest. The Scriptures are very helpful in this regard. If you know the words God has already said, it will help you figure out what "sounds like" Him—what types of things He is likely to want you to do as well as what He won't ask you to do. If what you "hear" does not absolutely cohere with Scripture, it is likely not from God. As you read through the Bible, you will find many filters to help you see what is from God and what isn't.

The better you know God, the more you will distinguish His voice from the rest.

If I feel driven by pride, guilt, or selfishness, I can likely conclude that what I am doing is not from God. God may use guilt to convict us of sin so that we will turn back to Him, but after that, guilt is not from God. That is the Devil's tool. God leads us with hope, peace, and a passionate motivation to love.

If you are looking for pat answers about how to distinguish the voice of God from the voice of the enemy, you will not find them. If you want to know the voice of God in your life, the only way to do that is to spend time with Him. Learn to sit still in His presence; spend time in His Word. This is one of the mistakes I made in the first few years of my ministry. I kept trying to find formulas for everything. I wanted a checklist for a good interview, a good meeting, a good counseling session. I wanted a rubric for church growth and financial development. A relationship with God must be dynamic, alive, not mechanistic. We can't just take it apart to see how it works and from that build a model of perfect godly relationships.

God is alive, and our relationship with Him must be able to mold, to move, and to change. God speaks to all of us in different ways, and so we need to spend enough time with Him so that we can hear Him when He has something to say.

The really clever thing about the game of Angels and Demons is that the demons could win simply by keeping people from the cabin/heaven. They didn't have to get people to the dumpster/hell. The Devil doesn't have to get you to walk into hell; he just has to keep you from walking through the gates of heaven.

> Enter through the narrow gate. For wide is the gate and broad is the road that leads to destruction, and many enter through it. But small is the gate and narrow the road that leads to life, and only a few find it. (Matt. 7:13–14)

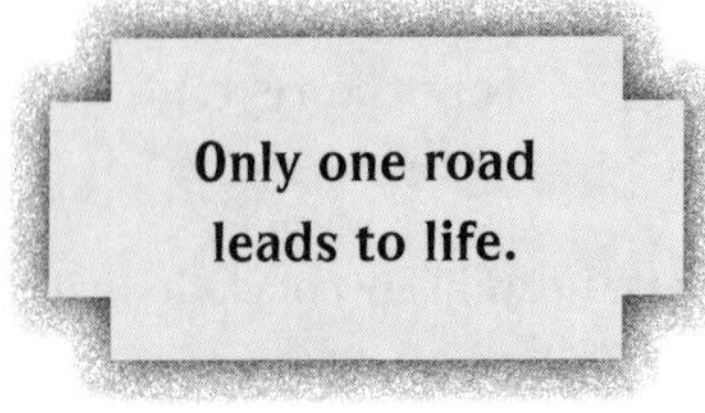

Only one road leads to life. All the Devil has to do is keep you off the one narrow road. He can use other religions, an improper focus, money, responsibility, family, friends, and any number of other tactics to keep you from walking down the road that leads to life. He's dangerous, not because of how powerful he is, but because he can lead you astray, and most of us don't put up much of a fight.

Think about Jesus' temptation (Matt. 4; Luke 4). The Devil comes to Jesus after He has fasted for forty days. To say that Jesus was hungry would be an understatement. Jesus was starving, and if He didn't eat soon, He would die. So what does the Devil tempt Him with? Food. The Devil tries to get Jesus to make bread. What's wrong with that? (Now, instead of the nasty guy you picture in hearing the word "devil," picture a concerned mother. *Aww, honey, you've got to eat something!*) Jesus is starving; He can't accomplish His mission if He starves to death. A few chapters later, He'll perform a similar miracle. It'll both demonstrate His power *and* fulfill a need He has. (And how can you say no to *Mom*?) Everything seems to justify this action.

It's important to see that the Devil isn't tempting Jesus to sin, to break a commandment. He is tempting Jesus to take a shortcut. Despite good reason and a seemingly innocent proposal, Jesus, thankfully, does not give in to instant self-gratification. I can't even imagine that. Forty days without food and He still has the willpower not only to avoid sin but to avoid taking the easy way out. Unbelievable.

Do you see what the Devil is doing? Jesus came to earth for a reason. He went into the wilderness to fast for a reason. Jesus is preparing to start His ministry, a ministry that will end in His death and the Devil's defeat. Jesus has an eternal purpose; He has a mission to accomplish. All the Devil wants to do is to get Jesus to focus on His present hunger, His current need and not the future, not the kingdom.

We often write this off too quickly. "Of course Jesus resisted," we say. "He is after all God." Yet we forget that He is also man. Jesus did not resist the Devil's temptation because He was God; if that were the case, this story would not benefit us and there would hardly be a reason to record it. Jesus resisted the Devil because He kept focused on God's mission and would not allow Himself to be distracted, even by overwhelming physical hunger. That is how we resist temptation. We focus our attention on God and we don't let anything distract us. The Devil will not always tempt us with blatant sin, but he may use an innocent distraction that leads to sin, which is far more insidious.

Even a focus on not sinning is a distraction!

Even a focus on *not sinning* is a distraction! Every second we spend worrying about not sinning or focused on resisting sin is a second in which we are not focused on God. So the problem is, when we have a habitual sin in our lives, we often focus on trying to figure out how to avoid that sin rather than focusing on strengthening our relationship with God. We spend more time distracted with breaking down old, bad habits than we do trying to build new, good habits. Even when we are successful, we fail. You cannot have victory if you don't fight the right battles.

God is not asking for our attempts at sinlessness. He is asking for us to love Him. If the Devil can allow our good intentions to keep us from that relationship with God that truly transforms us, then he can use good intentions to keep us from doing what we should be doing.

There is at least one thing we can know about the Devil: he is crafty.

Ambushed

In the eyes of our enemy, a Zombie church is the perfect place to ambush believers.

Have you ever noticed that when you are driving and you look off to the side of the road at something, you slowly start to drift in the direction you are looking? That's because you naturally move in the direction your vision is focused. So when your eyes are focused on the road (God), you naturally stay on track. If, however, you look off to your right at a billboard (distraction) for too long, you will find yourself drifting into the next lane or off the road altogether.

In a Zombie church, where the church has lost its singular focus on Jesus, and does not continually put Jesus before the people, the Devil finds it easier to distract us. Unlike the feeling you would get when driving off a road in your car, we can journey off the correct path on our spiritual journey without much noticeable change.

> **The church is where our enemy does some of his best work.**

It is hard to focus on what we cannot see when there is so much right in front of us that we can see. We often miss the spiritual world because of the distractions in the physical one. How easy it is to be distracted in church or during prayer! "I can't believe what she's wearing . . . talk about skanky." "That guy doesn't sing during worship. I guess he doesn't love Jesus." "Oh look, the lady who gives everyone mean looks is here; I wish she wasn't such a hypocrite." The church is where our enemy does some of his best work.

> Jesus told them another parable: "The kingdom of heaven is like a man who sowed good seed in his field. But while everyone was sleeping, his enemy came and sowed weeds among the wheat, and went away. When the wheat sprouted and formed heads, then the weeds also appeared.
>
> "The owner's servants came to him and said, 'Sir, didn't you

> sow good seed in your field? Where then did the weeds come from?'
>
> "'An enemy did this,' he replied.
>
> "The servants asked him, 'Do you want us to go and pull them up?'
>
> "'No,' he answered, 'because while you are pulling the weeds, you may root up the wheat with them. Let both grow together until the harvest. At that time I will tell the harvesters: First collect the weeds and tie them in bundles to be burned; then gather the wheat and bring it into my barn.'" (Matt. 13:24–30)

This parable is not a portrait of the world but of the church. The wheat represents the people of God and yet among them grow weeds. Those weeds can damage the crop, but they also tend to distract the workers. So our enemy focuses our minds on the condition and sins of others to keep us from finding them in ourselves. We are not right. Our souls have been tainted with an illness while we are distracted by trivial things. Surely you have felt this in your own life. You have felt disappointment in the actions or attitude of another Christian while neglecting to look at yourself.

Do you think it any wonder that our minds so easily wander while we are in church? Why does the person singing off key keep us from worshipping God? Are you surprised that your worship of God is affected by how you feel about the quality of the music? You shouldn't be. This happens in a church that has lost its focus. When the church is alive and well, on the other hand, then the Devil has a harder time distracting you. When you have the proper motivation and focus, when you are surrounded by people who love and care for you, and when you are equipped with the right weapons to defend against the Devil's attacks, then you are in a position of strength. That doesn't mean the Devil can't get to you, but why make his job easy? Focusing our attention on God and investing in godly relationships with godly people is a powerful defense against the attack of the enemy. When you are surrounded by the truth, the Devil's lies are a much harder sell.

It is easier to follow rules than it is to follow the Spirit of the living God.

In Zombie churches, religious things keep us from spiritual things. By this I mean that there is a natural life and energy that comes from the Spirit of God. When that Spirit is present, we feel it and it is powerful. When the Spirit leaves, rather than pursuing it we seek ways to fill the void of its absence. We turn to rituals as a default mode of operation. One thing is abundantly clear: it is easier to follow rules than it is to follow the Spirit of the living God.

When the church is alive, it naturally moves and grows. When the church fails to follow the movement of the Spirit, we try to turn a living organism into a functional machine. We get concerned over music style, the order of service, the image of the cross, the appearance of others, doctrine, technicalities, and controversies, and are oblivious to the fact that God is not in these things. The danger of this is that we think ourselves spiritually-minded while remaining spiritually blind.

Look at the story of King Saul and King David. King Saul grieved the Spirit of God when he offered a sacrifice while impatiently waiting for Samuel. He felt pressured and tried to rush God into action. Saul's response to this realization was short of repentance. So Saul lost favor with God and would ultimately lose his throne (1 Sam. 15). King David, though described as "a man after God's own heart," also grieved the Spirit of God when he slept with Bathsheba and had her husband murdered to cover up his affair (2 Sam. 11–12).

The difference between Saul, who was a zombie, and David whose heart was alive with God is that when David realized what he had done, he repented. When we grieve the Spirit of God, we must aggressively, tenaciously, immediately deal with the problem. Going through the motions doesn't cut it. David sinned and turned back to God. This is the only cure for the zombie condition. We cannot fake it or play at church and have true life. The soul of the church must remain in connection with the soul of God, which is the Holy Spirit.

Soul Focus

In order to keep ourselves safe from the deceit and distractions, we need to do two things: The first is that we need to make ourselves familiar with God's Word. This enables us to discern between lies and the truth of God. Second, we need better perspective. Some truths are not worth fighting over and some are not worth dividing over. Sometimes a little truth can be a distraction from more important truth. We need to realize what is important and what isn't.

I preached a sermon one Sunday, and in one of my points I was talking about how churches have started prioritizing theological differences over saving the lost. Thousands of people are dying and going to hell every day. While God's work goes unfinished, churches are just sitting around arguing amongst themselves as to which of them is the most right in the kingdom of God. We need to stop arguing over theological differences that do not pertain to salvation—like instruments on stage or speaking in tongues.

We had a visitor that Sunday who cornered me after the service and began to lecture me about the error of what I had said. Now, I am more than capable of making mistakes and try to be open to hearing about them when they happen, so I listened intently to his objection. He was saying that speaking in tongues is not real, that the perfect had come and tongues have ceased, so I shouldn't have said it was not important to argue about. Again, regardless of your perspective on tongues in Scripture, he totally missed the point.

The road may be narrow, but sometimes in the church we are guilty of making it even narrower than it really is.

The point is, the church needs to stop arguing over things that do not affect salvation. Can you believe in speaking in tongues and go to heaven? Yes. Can you deny speaking in tongues and go to heaven? Yes. So is this something worth arguing about when the church has more important work to do, like bringing lost people to a relationship with Jesus?

This is really the soul of the problem. When Jesus talks about the narrow way, He is not referring to a single denomination that gets all the answers right. He is referring to people (from many different denominations) who get the relationship with Him right. The road may be narrow, but sometimes in the church we are guilty of making it even narrower than it really is.

We have this tendency to think that heaven will be only for us and for people who agree with our "biblical" position. The narrow road Jesus spoke of is not about heavenly population control (keeping people out who follow Jesus differently than we do) but a statement about how few will get the relationship right. Narrow means Jesus is the only way. Sometimes we treat church as a spiritual competition. The team that gets the most answers right gets in and everyone else is out of luck.

Sometimes we focus too much on the narrow road and too little on 2 Peter 3:9, which says that God is not willing that any should perish but desires that everyone would come to repentance. God wants everyone to be saved. He established the church to help make that desire a reality. As Christians we exist to share the life of God with the world. Will we always be successful? No. But do we already have the victory? Yes. Eternity is at stake and we have been called by God to take the good news of His Son to the world. We need to live our lives as if nothing could stop us from completing that mission.

If we learn anything from 1 Corinthians 8, it should be that it is not the one with the most accurate interpretation of every Scripture who pleases God; it's the one who, seasoned with love and grace, positively influences others toward heaven. That's the one who pleases God. In the end love is all that remains, which makes love the most worthy investment of our lives.

We need to stop focusing all our attention on teaching the ninety-nine to do neat tricks in the safety of the pasture.

Remember Jesus' story of the lost sheep? Ninety-nine were in the pasture and the shepherd left all of them behind to go look for the one that was lost (Matt. 18; Luke 15). Lost people have a special place in the heart of God, and the church really has neglected the people that God cares about. Here is the truth: God is not denominational and He is not a theologian. This life is not about getting as many answers right as you can; it is about loving God as much as you can. Which means taking care of the hurting, seeking the lost, going out into the world and showing the love of God to others. There is more rejoicing for the one lost sheep that is found than for the ninety-nine that were never lost. We need to stop focusing all our attention on teaching the ninety-nine to do neat tricks in the safety of the pasture. We need to go out to find the lost one. That is a shepherd who seriously cares for his sheep. (God was the originator of the "no man left behind" motto.)

I want to be clear here. I am not saying theological issues are not important. Nor am I saying we should not spend time studying them, even discussing them. It is important for us to be educated and to know what we believe on theological issues. What I am saying is that we must learn to keep those issues in proper perspective. Are they worth dividing the church over? Are they worth damaging a brother's faith over? There is still work to be done, and the church has better things to do than sit around and fight. We need to stop putting theology above God.

We need to stop putting theology above God.

It is like we forget that *the Creator of heaven and earth wants to have a relationship with us!* Something needs to change. What if the churches stopped arguing about God and started seeking a deeper relationship with God? What if we just tried to focus on Him and nothing else? Can you imagine what the world would look like? If we made Jesus the sole focus of our lives; if He was the center, the foundation, the keystone of all that we are? Can you imagine what the church would look like? One of the most common problems outsiders have with the church is our hypocrisy. I believe the primary thing they see as hypocrisy is that we spend all this time talking about God and very little time trying to look and act like Him.

When the soul is missing, people are content in living around others who are missing the same things they are. The problem comes when

When we encounter someone with passion for Jesus in the church, we often try to calm them down, to control the fire, and eventually even to put it out.

someone who has life walks into a church of the undead. The passion of new Christians often roars like a wildfire, as they desperately search for more of God in their lives. And their passion and desire offends those who have lost it. These "mature" Christians sometimes give really bad advice: "You know, this is just a wave and it will crash one day." Think about surfers. They paddle out into the ocean and a wave comes. They ride the wave and it crashes. When that happens, they don't pull their boards onto the beach and say, "Bummer, that's over." No way! They turn around, paddle back out, and wait for the next wave. Sometimes we give this advice with good intention, but it is advice that suppresses life.

When a Christian's passion burns brightly, we worry they will burn out fast. This is a fair concern with a campfire, where the source of fuel is limited. But we need to remember what Moses learned about the burning bush: the flame of God doesn't burn out. When we encounter someone with passion for Jesus in the church, we often try to calm them down, to control the fire, and eventually even to put it out. That is what the religious leaders tried to do to Jesus, and that is what the church still tries to do to those who share in His fanatic lifestyle.

Undead churches want undead people, because when you're surrounded with people just like you, you don't feel guilty for being the way you are. If you were a racist, for example, you would want to surround yourself with other racists so you can be what you are without any guilt or call to change. If, however, you were around someone who realizes that your nationality or skin color do not make you better or worse as a person, even if they don't say anything, the gracious way they live would be a constant testimony to the flaws in your life.

It seems almost ironic that a great part of the cure for the undead is to find life. Drawing so close to God that He is a part of everything you do, connecting with Him so personally that your thoughts and attitudes reflect His—this is what it means to find life. You don't make personal decisions, you make biblical decisions. You don't have a selfish focus, you focus on Christ in everything. "Bad company corrupts good character" (1 Cor. 15:33); the company of Jesus brings life. The more you spend time with Him, the more His life becomes a part of yours. So much so that it becomes no stretch to say "the LORD is your life" and "Christ . . . is your life" (Deut. 30:20; Col. 3:4).

There is a Christian organization that puts on big events for young Christians all over the country. Growing up I was amazed at how powerful and significant this organization was, and even dreamed of working with them in some form or another. A good friend of mine worked there, and when we would talk about his job, I began to see a problem. My friend felt very disconnected while he was there. Everyone did their own thing and, for the most part, ignored him. When he was going through a hard time, none of his co-workers were really there to support him, even when he asked for it.

Zombies need to destroy life.

A young woman who worked there used to bake cookies or brownies every night and bring them into work so people could enjoy them the next day. She expressed her love for people that way. After a few weeks her boss told her that she had to stop bribing people to be her friends. This Christian organization—that teaches young people about the love of Jesus—discouraged showing that love in the workplace. One girl doing something extra, bringing life to the company, made those who were droning through the week uncomfortable.

A single person who has life can bring life to an entire church, but oftentimes that will be a long, difficult battle. If someone tries to bring life into a Zombie church, they are often met with hostility. Zombies need to destroy life. That's what they do. To be honest, that is sometimes what we do in the church. We sacrifice passion and zeal for the sake of conformity or uniformity. We try to package Christianity into this heartless, soulless, mindless box so no one has to work too hard and no one will be uncomfortable, because zombies don't feel anything.

If we are going to get life back in the churches, we have to stop trying to control and contain the people we come in contact with who are living the fanatic life of Jesus. We need to stop turning the passionate people into emotionally barren ones and instead let their life have an impact on others.

We must learn to know God both as individuals and as the church if we are ever going to get our soul back. Knowing God and following after Him: this is the purpose of the church. He is the reason for its existence and the center of everything it does. A living church does not concern itself with personal glory, fame, or even recognition. They simply seek more of God. They understand that the greatest thing, the only real refreshment, nourishment, and satisfaction we can really encounter in this world is just knowing God.

All it takes is one: one person who sets Jesus as their focus. One person dedicated totally to Him. One person willing to follow Jesus whatever the cost. One person who has life. The life of one can give life to many. It is not always easy, but it is always worth it. Maybe that person is you. Maybe the reason you find yourself in a church of zombies is so you can be an instrument of life in that community. One person so connected to Christ that the love of Jesus flows out may be a cure to an entire church community.

Chapter Seven

THE ROTTEN MIND

In *The Signal* (2007),[1] a mysterious transmission, broadcast over every form of electronic device, turns normal people into killers. The people are not ravenous, but something about the signal sends them into a mindless zombielike rage. Losing all reason and logic, they are filled with intense feelings of jealousy, fear, and hatred. This maddening signal devastates most of the world's population. It seems that when the barriers of the mind start coming down, people start behaving in ways completely uncharacteristic of who they are.

In most films, one of the most defining features of zombies is that zombies are neither intelligent nor self-aware. They're likely to be unusually strong, but their minds are rotten and useless. Oh yes, and they tend to have a taste for the brains of the living. These mindless creatures are driven to devour the living. Why don't they go after each other? Hmm . . . this has an interesting parallel in the church.

Genuine life is an affront to zombies. Those who do not have true life seem hell-bent on destroying those who do. Perhaps it is because the undead know that the living can restore life. It seems like some people prefer being dead to being alive (apparently there are few expectations), so they set out to destroy anyone who has true life in order to prevent their comfortable lack-of-life from becoming uncomfortable.

Heart, Soul, *Mind*

"Love the Lord your God with all your heart and with all your soul and with all your *mind* . . ." (Matt. 22:37).

Our mind is what enables us to determine the will of God and to distinguish between good and evil. As it produces our thoughts and determines our attitudes, the mind is the source of our spiritual development. Maturity comes as we become less and less dependent on ourselves and more and more dependent on God—the result of changes that take place in our mind.

There is a context in which a gross lack of knowledge can be accurately construed as a lack of love, and that context is *relationship.*

Imagine this: my wife comes home and she asks me if I know what today is. I respond with no. She then gets understandably upset because I forgot our anniversary. Bad news, right? (Thankfully, this is hypothetical.)

Now imagine that my wife discovers that I don't know her favorite food, her favorite music, her favorite pastime. What's more, I don't know where she works or what she does for a living. I don't even know her likes and dislikes, her birthday, her middle name, or how many siblings she has. What would you think of me as a husband? A deadbeat! What kind of husband doesn't know anything about his wife? The sheer volume of my lack of knowledge about her might lead you to believe I don't really love her. There is a context in which a gross lack of knowledge can be accurately construed as a lack of love, and that context is *relationship.* What would happen if we examined our relationship with God in this light? Would you know God's favorite pastime? Where He's working? His likes and dislikes?

For many of us if our love for God was measured by what we knew about

Him, it would be pretty minuscule. Our rotting minds do not know God like we should. Whether it is your love for God that motivates you to get to know Him or your knowing Him that increases your love for Him, the result is the same: knowing and loving are inseparable in a real relationship. This does not mean that in order to love God you must be a scholar. By now, because of our discussion of *yada* in chapter 6, you realize that knowing God with our minds means much more than being really good at Bible trivia. (Don't we wish it was that easy!) No, knowing God is about taking the time to see His heart and to follow it.

I had a good friend in college who would often sit outside to watch the sunset. He was a brilliant and busy guy, but he liked to just sit and marvel at the greatness of God. I think he was onto something.

In our churches there is a condition that besets us. Our minds have started rotting away. Why do you think so many just abandon church when there are problems? We realize that *purpose* is gone, but we don't know how to get it back because our mind is gone too. Pursuing a knowledge of God is the responsibility of every person, not just the church leadership. We have neglected spending time in relationship with God and as a result the church has lost its life and become a decaying, undead version of its former self. We need to heal our minds so that we may see the cure to our lost soul.

For the most part in the church today, we have failed to know God intimately. We have failed to invest in Him through things like spending time in studying the Word, in meditation, in worship, in prayer, in service, or just sitting in awe of how great He is.

Illiterate

There is this growing problem of biblical illiteracy in the church. There was a time when preachers could mention a biblical character's name and safely assume almost all of their people were very familiar with that character. Today, we have to spend ten or fifteen minutes just introducing the character before ever getting into the story.

This could indicate something positive: if we are reaching unreached people, then it is wonderful that we have to explain more of the background of Bible stories and characters. Sadly, I'm not convinced that's the primary reason. It seems that in recent years there has been a decrease in the focus on the importance of knowing God through studying the Word. Memorizing Scripture in particular has taken a notable hit in modern culture. With quick-and-easy resources, such as Internet access on our mobile phones, the felt need to have the Word of God hidden in our hearts has been reduced. Here is the caveat: if you don't know that something exists, you won't know how to find it, and you won't even think to try to find it. Modern technology may appear to have reduced the need for memorization, but without diligent study of the Scriptures, the technology won't help us.

Trying to know God without knowing His Word is like trying to make a friend without actually listening to what the person says.

I have met seasoned Christians (I deliberately say *seasoned* rather than *mature*) who do not know the difference between the Old Testament and the New Testament. I have met seasoned Christians who couldn't tell you the names of the four Gospels. Although I've emphasized that knowing God is not only knowing about God, a certain degree of knowing comes from knowing about. If our knowing about, which can be clearly measured, is not very good, then it is reasonable to conclude that we do not know God as well as we should. How can we know God without knowing what He says? If you want to know someone, you spend time talking with them. The Bible is one of God's primary ways of communicating with us. Trying to know God without knowing His Word is like trying to make a friend without actually listening to what the person says.

After a number of years of following Christ, we should be at least somewhat familiar with the basics. An elementary school teacher was very active and involved at our church. One day, she was talking about how she struggled with reading the Bible because she had read it when she was a kid and felt she knew the stories. She had all but stopped reading the Bible because it was "old news." If we flip past stories or read over events because we are somewhat familiar with them, however, we can miss what God is trying to say to us now. We miss out on a more mature understanding of the meaning of those events.

Our lack of knowledge of God's Word results in two things: first, a lack of understanding of God, since His Word is one of the primary ways in which He reveals Himself to us, and second, a lack of maturity. The author of Hebrews is frustrated with his audience for this very reason:

> We have much to say about this, but it is hard to explain because you are slow to learn. In fact, though by this time you ought to be teachers, you need someone to teach you the elementary truths of God's word all over again. You need milk, not solid food! Anyone who lives on milk, being still an infant, is not acquainted with the teaching about righteousness. But solid food is for the mature, who by constant use have trained themselves to distinguish good from evil.
>
> Therefore let us leave the elementary teachings about Christ and go on to maturity, not laying again the foundation of repentance from acts that lead to death, and of faith in God. (Heb. 5:11–6:1)

Nothing can replace the importance of God's Word. What we are reading is not just ancient words on a page but God's instruction manual for us. Far from a pointless endeavor or mindless discipline, the reading of God's Word shows us how to live. The Bible is the food for our souls. It is vital to our lives. In its pages we find life. It tells us of the law of God that we have broken. It tells us of the love of God in sending His Son to redeem us from our sin. It tells us how to live our new redeemed life. If we don't know it, how can we allow it to change our lives? If we don't know it, how can we share with others?

So many are led astray by false teaching because they don't know the truth well enough to recognize a lie. We must develop a good habit of biblical intake. We won't see the Word of God coming out of our lives unless we are faithful to put it in.

Mindless

Paul shows us the importance of the Word of God in our lives:

> My purpose is that they may be encouraged in heart and united in love, so that they may have the full riches of complete understanding, in order that they may know the mystery of God, namely, Christ, in whom are hidden all the treasures of wisdom and knowledge. (Col. 2:2–3)

Do you see Paul's desire? He wants the church to experience the full riches of complete understanding. We come to an understanding of God in different ways, one of which is Bible study, but there has to be more than that. The religious leaders of Jesus' day knew their Scriptures front, back, sideways, and inside out. The problem was, they knew the Scripture but they did not know Jesus.

When I first went to Ozark Christian College, I thought I was the greatest thing to happen to the kingdom of God since Pentecost. I had been active in my youth group, I prided myself on being a very intelligent person, and so I thought it was going to be a cakewalk. I had thoughts and opinions about the Bible based on things I had heard over the years, and I was just sure I was going to blow the professors' minds. I had really intelligent sounding answers for everything. Oh, if only I'd known how foolish I really was.

My first semester I was in a class on the book of Acts, and I had to write a paper on speaking in tongues. I wrote a twenty-page exegetical paper analyzing and explaining speaking in tongues and giving my absolute and authoritative thoughts on it. When I turned my paper in, I thought about saying "You're welcome" to my professor since he was being given this gift of reading my brilliant work. Then I got the paper back. Entire sentences were crossed out, paragraphs, one page had a giant red X through it with a note to the side that said: "You didn't say anything here." Written in multiple places was the phrase: "Blah blah blah." He had more corrections than I had valid thoughts.

That professor may never know the effect he had on my life. He taught me how to think. He taught me that opinions are not facts. There are a lot of people who want their fiction to be accepted as fact. Loving God with our minds does not mean reading a passage and deciding what it means based on how *we* feel about it. Loving God with our minds means seeking the truth of what *God* is really saying, regardless of our thoughts, desires, and feelings. When it comes to Scripture, you didn't write it, so your interpretation of it is neither absolute nor authoritative.

The Bible was not written *to* you, but it was written *for* you.

Reading the Bible is a lot like reading a journal. We see statements and emotions being expressed, but in order to truly understand them, we need to know what was going on when they were written. Flipping open to some random page will not give us context. We must not read the Bible as if it was written to us, because it wasn't. Instead, start at the beginning. Learn the history that leads up to what you read so you can understand what's going on. What led up to this point? What was going on at the time this was written? We need to understand Scripture as a whole by reading it in context.

When we read Scripture out of context, we misconstrue its meaning. We latch onto promises from God that are not intended as promises, or not intended for us. This can ruin lives, because when the promise that was not truly understood goes unfulfilled, God's faithfulness and even His existence and love are thrown into question. A lot of the bad theology and problematic biblical views that exist are a result of people reading the Bible as if it was written to them. The Bible was not written *to* you, but it was written *for* you. Even Christians in the first century needed to understand this, which is why Paul explained *to* them and *for* us, "Everything that was written in the past was written to teach us, so that through endurance and the encouragement of the Scriptures we might have hope" (Rom. 15:4).[2] So we read and observe what is written, interpret it and apply it to our lives, and then those archaic words written to strangers long ago become personal words where God speaks to you.

Unappealing

Getting to know God through the written Word has lost its appeal. Reading the Bible has stopped being a privilege and started becoming a chore. The Word of Life given to us as a gift from God has become little more than words on a page speaking to a people too preoccupied to listen. As our culture chases after more and more entertainment, the power of words on a page is waning. But the Bible is *more than words on a page.* The Bible is our touchstone for truth and a part of God's revelation of Himself. Yet nowadays the Bible is a casualty of Zombie churches, albeit a well-intentioned one.

For years I listened to preachers talking and complaining about how we don't read the Bible enough. They talked about the "discipline of Bible reading," and they set tangible standards for the amount of time we should spend reading our Bible every day. Perhaps it's just me, but when reading the Bible became a discipline, it started to feel a lot like an obligation. Now, I know that it's very important to invest in that kind of study even when I don't feel like it. The problem I have is that when it feels like an obligation, I don't get much joy out of it. In fact, under those conditions, it was easy to become resentful at the idea of reading Scripture because the guilt of not fulfilling the obligation was overwhelming.

No monologue about the importance of reading Scripture preached from a man looking down on me from behind a pulpit was going to change this feeling. What I needed was not an external motivator but an internal one. The solution was not hearing someone else tell me how important reading a book was. The solution was having someone help introduce me to the One who wrote it. If you force me to read something, I will do so begrudgingly, but give me a love note from my wife, and I will read it again and again. I will hold on to it, treat it as precious, and pour over every word. What we need is not more Nike-commercial Christians who "just do it," but we need people to see the heart of God in His letter for us.

A friend of mine introduced me to a preacher who was posting his sermons on YouTube. It was one of the funniest things I had ever heard—except for how horrible it was. This guy was yelling and screaming the whole time about all sorts of nonsense, such as how if you don't use the King James Bible, you are going to hell. He bragged about how much he read the Bible and how many verses he memorized, and he said that if the people were not reading their Bible faithfully all the time, then God would judge them for it. I am all for tough love, but this guy was forcefully trying to guilt-trip people into reading the Word. Now thankfully, preachers like this are not all that common, and yet we've all seen or heard of one.

The sad thing is that we respond inappropriately when we hear this kind of message. We miss the real point. We hear that reading the Word of God is an obligation. Guilt. We hear that if we don't read it, we are bad Christians, and God won't love us anymore. Guilt. We hear that God's love is conditional.

Guilt motivates different people differently, but we all want to get rid of it. For some, guilt removes any desire to read the Bible in the future, since the Bible has become the source of great pain in our lives. Then we go on to become bitter and frustrated because we don't really understand what reading our Bible is all about. Whether you've read your Bible today or not, God doesn't love you any less (or more) than He did yesterday. We don't read it to earn God's affection; we read it to get to know Him better.

Scripture refers to the Word of God as food for our soul. When you skip a meal, what do you feel? I first of all feel angry, because I love eating, and then, more importantly, hungry. In all my life I have never once felt guilty because I didn't eat something. If the Bible is our spiritual food, then when we fail to read it we shouldn't feel guilty; we should feel hungry! We should take a lesson from Moses:

> Moses said to the LORD, "You have been telling me, 'Lead these people,' but you have not let me know whom you will send with me. You have said, 'I know you by name and you have found favor with me.' If you are pleased with me, teach me your ways so

> I may know you and continue to find favor with you. Remember that this nation is your people."
>
> The LORD replied, "My Presence will go with you, and I will give you rest."
>
> Then Moses said to him, "If your Presence does not go with us, do not send us up from here. How will anyone know that you are pleased with me and with your people unless you go with us? What else will distinguish me and your people from all the other people on the face of the earth?" (Exod. 33:12–16)

Do you hear the cry of Moses' heart? He is pleading with God: "Let me know who you are!" He asks God to teach him that he may better understand. Why? Moses does not want to know God so he can loft his knowledge over others. He wants to know God better so he can continue to please Him. Moses' desire is to know God so he can continue to find favor with God.

Moses had a desire to know God intimately and to understand Him better. This passion is not an obligation. He has encountered the awesome power of God, and now Moses can think of nothing better than just to know God and to be known by Him. Moses recognizes something very important: he realizes that God knows him and yet that is not enough. He doesn't just want to be known: he wants to know God. What he is asking for is not rules; Moses is asking for a relationship.

The feeling we get when we don't spend that quality time getting to know God will tell us where our attitude really is. Guilt comes from treating knowing God as an obligation or rule. Hunger comes from treating knowing God as a vital part of life. The longer we go without the Word of God, the greater our desire for it should be. When we miss a day then we ought to crave it. When you get hungry enough, all you can think about is eating, satisfying the desire, that need in your life. This is how we ought to feel about the Word of God.

When you love someone, you naturally want to know all about them. The Bible is God's love letter to us. It is an important way that we get to know Him (though not the only way). If we truly loved God with all our minds, then the first thing we would do in the morning would be to get out of bed, grab our Bible, and dive into it with excitement and joy. We would pray with passion and with love, and we would spend time just watching to see what God might do in our lives that day. Then when we set that Bible down, we wouldn't move on to the next waffle-compartment of our life; we would move in step with God all day. We would walk with Him in everything we do. We would invite God to share breakfast with us; we would talk to Him while driving to work. He would be in our thoughts all day at work: "I can't wait until five. I can't wait until I get home so I can spend more uninterrupted time with God." Loving God with all of our minds means never being able to get enough of Him. It means constantly pursuing more knowledge, more understanding, more information.

Obsession

Zombie churches have created generations of Christians who have little desire for knowing God. Now the desire I'm talking about is not a verbal desire. Desire is not just about wanting something; it is about wanting something enough to do something about it. Sure, most people in the church will express a desire to know God better, but do they do anything about it? God is not playing hide-and-seek. He has promised you that if you seek Him, you will find Him. He is oftentimes just waiting for you to do the seeking so He can do the revealing.

> **Amen has taught us that the prayer is over.**

Amen means "truly, verily, so let it be." It is an affirmation of what is being said. I love *amen*, but I think it has had a negative effect on our relationship with God. *Amen* has taught us that the prayer is over. It separates our prayer life from the rest of our life. What would happen if we stopped ending prayers with *amen*?

Without a clear cutoff, prayer might just bleed over into other areas of our life. We might realize that prayer is a verb, not a noun. Prayer is a lifestyle. If we could learn to stop using *amen* as a closing statement in our communication with God, perhaps we could learn to spend every moment inviting God to be a part of it, living in a continual conversation with God. As long as we are awake, we could literally pray without ceasing.

My mom has an insatiable hunger for God. It doesn't matter what's going on, she always finds a way to start talking about God. She will call just to check up and see how we are doing, and somehow we get into a half-hour conversation about God. She will connect anything you say to something she is learning about God.

She will unashamedly change any subject that is not about God into a subject that is. Her passion, her heart, her desire is just to know God and to spend time with Him. It is an obsession—one we should all imitate. When she spends time with God, she goes in a room and locks the rest of the world away so she can have time alone with Him. She does this every day.

Although there are some great examples of people who love God with their entire mind, they are rare enough that we view them as weird. Rather than the church's social outcasts, they should be our trendsetters.

I went to a Christian elementary school. In class our teachers would give us time for Bible reading. They gave us highlighters to mark what we read so we could remember it. I misunderstood. I went through and just started highlighting line by line, page by page. My goal was to get from start to finish highlighted. Why? So that from start to finish would be highlighted.

Sometimes this is how we read the Bible: without purpose. We read it to read it. Not to learn. Not to understand. Not to see what God is saying to us through His Word preserved through the ages for us, but just to read it. We go through the Bible-in-a-year plans to read the Bible, but for what? There is nothing wrong with trying to read through the Bible or even to do it in a year, but there are more important things than just reading it. Would it be better to know every word written in Scripture or to understand key verses well?

We need to stop trying to reach a quota or to get through the Bible in a timely fashion and start really spending time with the Text. We need to quit thinking that reading over the Bible will make us better Christians. You could read the Bible cover to cover a thousand times and not be any closer to God than when you started. You can actually get more out of a single verse if you take the time to sit down and meditate on it. Think of it as a nice steak: before you digest it, you have to chew on it for a while. If you're a vegetarian, picture a bowlful of fresh crunchy vegetables: same thing, start chewing! If we want to avoid the problem of rotten minds, we have to learn not just to read the Word of God but to obsess over it.

It's Alive!

My wife and I started doing a Bible study on Galatians. I took a class on this book in college where I was required to read it in six different translations. I've done various other projects on Galatians and have preached from it a few times. I've read through this book a lot. So I honestly didn't expect to learn anything new from it.

As we read, however, I noticed a verse that I had read a dozen times before and had never really paid that much attention to. For some reason, this time it stuck out at me. I began to think about this verse and then started studying it, and suddenly this passage came to life and I found meaning and depth that I had not seen before.

The Bible is more than words on a page—it is God's living Word to us. In it, we find answers for the problems we wrestle with today. Incredibly, it is always relevant.

The Bible is more than words on a page—it is God's living Word to us.

In reading the Bible, something that has helped me is to approach the Bible every time as if it were the first time. Although you may have read the words before, you have never read those words at this precise point in your life before. Daily your life changes: your circumstances change, your needs change, your knowledge, understanding, and emotions change. Perhaps a passage that was nothing more than words on a page for twenty years did not connect to you because you were not ready, but at this moment in time, as you are reading this passage you have read countless times in the past, all of a sudden God will speak to you through it. If you will come to the text with a humble heart, you might be amazed at how it speaks to you. I recommend starting off with this little prayer:

> God, I'm opening Your Word. You said this Word is living and active. You wrote it for our benefit. You said, ask for wisdom, and You'll give it. I'm asking: help me to be aligned with *You*. Show me what You want me to get from this. I don't trust my reason, opinions, feelings. I am submitting to *Your* superior mind. God, I want to know You. Please show Yourself to me as I read, so that I may continue to find favor in Your sight.

That is what happened with me while studying Galatians. I had read the words so many times before, but in seeing it at the right moment in my life, it became clear and those words came alive and spoke to me. It was incredible!

God gives us insights into Scripture the same way parents give gifts to their children. Picture a little boy getting his first Matchbox car. He plays with it all the time, making car noises as he races it around the house. When the boy gets a little older, maybe his parents get him a remote control car. This is a whole new level of awesome for the little boy who excitedly plays with his new toy. As the child gets a little older, perhaps he gets power wheels, then a four-wheeler; finally, when he reaches an age of maturity, a car. Each gift is great for the child at each age and stage. As the child matures, the gifts get better and better. This is how we should read Scripture. As we mature, the truths that God communicates to us are richer, more valuable, and more significant in our lives. Each gift is good, but the goal should be to reach that point of maturity where we can appreciate the fullness of the truth of Scripture in our lives. Reading Scripture should be like Christmas. Sure, you have had it before, but each time around it proves to be a new adventure and another special gift to unwrap.

Now I'm not saying that God hides meaning from us on all texts, or even that He hides all the meaning of any text, but that the depth of meaning that brings some texts to life may be concealed until we are ready to receive it. To me this is fitting when we consider the parables of Jesus. A parable is designed to do two things: to reveal something and to conceal something. Sometimes Jesus told parables to keep people from understanding the kingdom of God because they weren't ready. That's why we often see Him explaining His parables to the disciples later.

Yet before He explains, you know what we often see? We see the disciples asking for an explanation. Perhaps the difference between those who are ready to understand the kingdom of God and those who are not is as simple as being willing to honestly ask questions. It really is like the Word of God is a treasure that needs a key to unlock it, and our study and relationship with Him gives us access to more of those keys to unlock more of those texts so that we may better know Him.

It is like a relationship. You don't share the intimate secrets of your life with a stranger. As time moves on and that stranger becomes an acquaintance, you feel more comfortable and let them see a bit more of who you are. Over time, when you see their heart and you learn that they are trustworthy, then you start to share the depths of who you are with them.[3] Every text has a surface meaning that anyone can see, but as we grow in our understanding of God, we start moving through the newly unlocked doors, finding hidden truths that for us bring His Word to life.

It can be scary and overwhelming to try to get to know God on your own, so don't.

When we learn to see the Bible for what it is—not a chore to be done but a treasure to be pursued—we begin to utilize our minds in the process. God's desire is not for us to recognize that He is God; He is not so insecure as to need that reinforcement of His identity. God's desire is for us to pursue Him and to know Him. We cannot adequately do this without using our heads.

I realize that the task of knowing a God who is bigger than us is difficult, and without formal training in how to read the Word, we can sometimes lack the confidence to try. It can be scary and overwhelming to try to get to know God on your own, so don't. This is one of the purposes of the church: to help bring to life, in a variety of ways, this process of getting to know God. The church should study together, worship together, pray together, meditate together, serve together. A preacher's job really is not to entertain you; it is to help you understand the Word of God. A church's job is not to cater to your every need but to help you see what Jesus looks like.

The Zombie church with its rotted mind may be entertaining and engaging, but it won't develop your understanding of God. God gives us our minds so that we can appreciate His truth and His glory, and so we can respond to His revelation. The better you know God, the more you grow in a relationship with Him. When churches mindlessly go through motions, the people stop maturing and growing in their faith.

Having the Mind of God: Perspective

If you are reading the Bible because you feel like you should or you have to, I want you to do something: stop. Don't waste your time. Focus your attention on spending time with God in prayer or in some other way so that you can connect with Him on a personal level. The Bible is the story of God's love for us: it shouldn't be hard for us to find a desire to read and study it. Knowledge is important but it must be kept in its proper perspective. I sometimes have had to remind myself that knowledge is not God. I have respected the mind, often to the neglect of everything else, allowing my knowledge *of God* to interfere with my ability to love the people God loves. I made knowledge an idol and turned myself into a Pharisee. (If you haven't realized by now that I am by no means perfect, then this should prove it to you.) It's easy for too much knowledge to create a lifestyle filled with too little love, and it is better to err on the side of love.

Life does not come through knowledge. Life comes from a genuine relationship with Jesus Christ. Many amazing Christians whom I have come to respect are not very scholarly, but they have this wild devotion to Christ, who is the center of their lives. The challenge is really balancing knowledge with love. When knowledge is given an improper place in our lives, it creates division and disunity. I believe that's a leading cause of the different denominations that exist in the church today. If our primary focus had been love, we wouldn't have split into so many subgroups that can't play nice together.

Here again, I must say that this isn't a reason to abandon church but merely a problem to be corrected. There is a cure to the problem of a rotten mind: perspective. We need to stop looking at the Bible as homework that will earn us a good grade in righteous living and start seeing it as the wonderful adventure of the Christian life that each of us has been invited to be a part of. God sought us out and pursued us, and now our lives are the journey of getting to know Him.

To love God with all of our minds is to live in the state of seeking to know God better. It will change the way you read the Word, pray, worship, and . . . everything else. When you start looking at the Bible as a message that was preserved so you could read it—that God saved every verse that He did because He wants to tell you something—it changes the way you view the Word. Each word is a gift bought with the blood of those who came before us. In each word we can find the life that God designed for us to have. As you seek God, He will open your eyes to what He is saying to you, and He can begin to mold and shape you. When you start to let the Word come to life, then you will not feel guilty when you don't read it, you will feel an overwhelming passion to make sure you do.

Chapter Eight

ZOMBIE STRENGTH

In most zombie movies the undead are supernaturally (though inexplicably) strong. Impervious to pain, they will keep coming for you, even if you remove some of their limbs! They have great physical strength, and yet they are (more or less) easily overcome, because in losing their hearts, souls, and minds, they have lost the greater sources of strength. Zombies are strong but not as strong as they would be if they could tap into now unrealized potential they had when they were alive.

Zombies, though tough, make terrible brides.

And Zombie churches, with their undead hearts, lost souls, and rotten minds, cannot hope to be strong without tapping into their unrealized potential—found in God Himself. While it might seem good that zombies keep moving forward, even after loss of limb, there is a downside. Zombies, though tough, make terrible brides. The church is not just here to survive; we are the bride of Christ.

Heart, Soul, Mind . . . and *Strength*

"Love the Lord your God with all your heart and with all your soul and with all your mind . . ." (Matt. 22:37).

For the last few chapters we have been looking at elements from Matthew 22:37 and how they have decayed in our churches. Parallel passages in Mark 12:30 and Luke 10:27 add a fourth trait to this list: *strength*. A living church loves God heart, soul, mind, and strength.

Through inaction a living church can degenerate into a church of the undead. Do you know what happens to a lake with an inlet but no outlet? Bacteria and toxins begin to grow. Moving water naturally purifies itself, but without an outlet the water will begin to settle and become stagnant. This happens in the spiritual lives of both individuals and church bodies. If we get poured into but don't let anything out, we become stagnant and harmful "bacteria" grows in our lives. When we let Jesus in our lives but don't let Him flow out of us, we turn into cesspools.

Evangelism, service, and prayer are the natural overflow of a Christian's spiritual life. When we are growing properly and maturing in our relationship with Christ, these things happen naturally. That does not mean you will wake up one day on a street corner with a megaphone preaching to strangers, but you will find yourself sharing your faith with others. You naturally share the things that matter to you with the people who matter to you. When I proposed to my girlfriend and she said yes, one of the first things I did was go through my list of phone contacts and tell the good news to everyone I cared about. If your faith matters to you, you will share it with the people you care about.

Having experienced the salvation and deliverance from sin that Jesus offers (input), the early church was not shy about their faith because they believed that what they had was good news for the world. Motivated by their overwhelming gratitude to God for His love (right purpose), they excitedly shared the message of the cross (output) with anyone who would listen. Their desire was to lead everyone to a relationship with Christ.

We need to become conduits of God's love, using our lives to distribute His love to the world. To be streams of "living water"—not toxin-filled pools—to the world. Many churches know what they ought to do and still fail to do it because they have exchanged the power of God for the power of man.

Dismembered: Service

In the beginning God worked. He created the world and everything in it. Jesus, being in nature God, did not sit back and take life easy. He worked hard, traveling, preaching, and healing. Consequently, the apostles worked hard, carrying out the commission they were given by the Lord. Paul was on the run, beaten, imprisoned, and flogged while performing his ministry, making tents, writing epistles to the churches, teaching in the synagogues, and healing the sick. The early church fathers strained and labored in their ministries and writings against oppressive governments in order to bring the good news of the gospel to the world. Yet even in their time there were those who were zombies. Those who wanted to reap the benefits of the community but offered nothing in return. So what shall we say to those who do nothing? As Christians we are called members of the body of Christ. When high percentages of the church do nothing, what we have is a dismembered body. While the body may still be alive, it has lost a lot of its functionality. So what do we do with those who cause the church to be dismembered—missing an ear, minus an index finger, or worse?

Titles lead to entitlement. When we call ourselves Christians, sometimes we start feeling like that means we deserve something. Sometimes even the grace of God becomes a gift we believe we have a right to. And then we lose our motivation. We have the life of God, so what's the point of working? Over time the message can become stale and we can take it for granted.

The trouble we have in our Zombie churches is that we have too many Christian spectators. I watched a movie a few years ago called *We Were Soldiers*[1] starring Mel Gibson. The movie was about the Vietnam War where a group of elite American troopers was surrounded by two thousand North Vietnamese soldiers. One of the young Americans in the movie was a photographer, Joe Galloway (played by Barry Pepper), who had come along to take pictures. When the Vietnamese soldiers attacked the American lines,

Sergeant Major Basil Plumley (played by Sam Elliott) tosses the photographer a gun. "But sir," says Joe, "I'm a noncombatant." To which the sergeant major responds, "Ain't no such thing today, boy."

We need to wake up and realize that like it or not we're in this war.

We need to wake up and realize that like it or not we're in this war. We live in a battle between the kingdom of God and the kingdom of Satan. The souls of man are on the line. In this war there is no such thing as noncombatants. This isn't a football game where some of the players can spend the entire game on the bench; this is war—it takes all of our collective strength. Can you imagine what church would be like if everyone was involved, if every Christian took up the call to arms and went into battle in the name of our King? Imagine what we could do; what kind of influence we could have for the kingdom of God.

It doesn't take a big church to change the world. When the church—any church—acts like the church, with all of its body parts functioning, serving others in love, the world will take notice. When we carry out the commands of God from Christ, the head of the body, we validate our faith. Something as simple as following God's commands can be the difference between someone sharing eternity with Him or living forever without Him.

The call to follow Jesus is a call to action, to service. You are not joining a club, you are enlisting in the service. In every kingdom there is a king. When the king leaves instructions for his servants, they are expected to follow those instructions. We are the servants and God is the King. Sometimes we get our roles reversed and we think of ourselves as king, and God as the servant who exists to serve us and give us what we want. For some reason that never works. We are the servants and as such God has left us some instructions:

> Again, it will be like a man going on a journey, who called his servants and entrusted his property to them. To one he gave five talents of money, to another two talents, and to another one

> talent, each according to his ability. Then he went on his journey. The man who had received the five talents went at once and put his money to work and gained five more. So also, the one with the two talents gained two more. But the man who had received the one talent went off, dug a hole in the ground and hid his master's money. (Matt. 25:14–18)

In the Greco-Roman world, it would not have been uncommon for a servant to have considerable responsibility and authority in his master's house. Being a slave to a powerful master could make you more important than a commoner. So the master entrusts each of these servants with large sums of money. A talent weighed around fifty-eight to eighty pounds. Its value was directly dependent on the value of the material it consisted of. While we might not know the precise value of this talent, we know that it's a considerable sum. It would take a common worker about twenty years to earn a single talent.

In this parable, each servant is entrusted with a different amount, depending on his ability. The first two servants start working immediately to earn more money for their master. They obviously knew what their master was expecting when he returned. But *three* servants had been entrusted with a great responsibility. Why does the third servant do nothing?

I imagine him just sitting back while the other two servants run around working hard. As they work, he laughs at them, maybe even teases them a bit. After all, when the master is gone the servant should get a vacation, right?

After a long time the master comes back. The first two servants faithfully lived up to their master's expectations. Pleased by their faithfulness (not necessarily by how much they had made), he rewards them by letting them share in his happiness and increasing their responsibility. Thus we see the intrinsic principle from Luke 12:48: "from the one who has been entrusted with much, much more will be asked."

Then the third servant is called in to give a report of what he has done. The problem was he hadn't done anything. Standing before his master, this servant starts off by making excuses. He even gets so bold as to accuse his master of exploitation and being too demanding. If he tried and failed, he would have incurred the master's wrath. If he worked hard and was successful, he would see little fruit from his labor.

So why risk so much for so little reward? This servant fails to recognize his responsibility to carry out the work that he had been assigned. The fact is, it was gracious for the master to trust him with anything. No matter how many reasons this wicked servant gives, there is no excuse for inaction. He failed to do what he had been entrusted to do. So everything he had was taken from him. He was cast from the master's home and into a place where there is "weeping and gnashing of teeth"—a biblical description of hell.

Why don't we stand up against the evil and injustices of this world?

Now, we can look at this parable of the talents and shake our heads at that foolish servant all we want. We may wonder why he didn't get to work, but the bigger question is, why don't we? We are a lot like this wicked servant. We have been given resources from which we could do great things. But like this servant, we sit back and do nothing. Why don't we do anything? Why don't we stand up against the evil and injustices of this world? For the same reason this servant didn't. We don't really believe the master is coming back. It's that simple. This servant didn't think his master would return from his journey, so he didn't bother working, not even to put the money on loan with a banker.

He buried the talent, betting the master would not return. Bad bet. We may think him foolish, but this is the same bet we make every day. When we don't tell our co-workers about Christ. When we don't "risk our friendships" by sharing the gospel. When we don't stand up at our malls, on our street corners, or in our schools to proclaim the love of God to the world.

Death to Self: Evangelism

In order to live for Christ we must die to ourselves. This is true not just of big life events but also of everyday ones. Now, that may mean something different for all of us. (That is not to say that truth is relative.) God calls us to different things. You may not want to mow the grass, but because your roommate is tired after a long day, even though it's not your turn, you do it anyway. It may mean that you would like to enjoy a relaxing day off, but you choose to give that up because a friend is moving to a new house and asks for your help.

For me it was preaching. When I was in school, I wanted to go into marketing and make lots of money advertising products for big companies and getting people to buy them. I was terrified of public speaking (actually I still am), and the last thing in the world I wanted to do was stand up in a roomful of people and do something as important as preach the Word of God. Yet for some reason that is exactly what God called me to do. I fought with Him at first, but here I am today. The strange thing is, I love it. Getting here, however, required that I lay down my desires for my life and submit myself to what God was asking me to do.

For you, perhaps dying to yourself is as simple as serving your spouse even when you don't feel like it. Or maybe you *could* win the argument—because of your superior debating skills—but instead of competing to win, you chose to listen respectfully. Perhaps denying yourself is treating people with a kindness they do not deserve. One thing is certain: dying to yourself means you are treating God and others as more valuable than yourself.

Dying to yourself is living a life that preaches the gospel without words—*lifestyle evangelism* we used to call it. It is showing people Jesus' love by how you treat them, not just telling them about it. If the price for unity with Christ is death, are we willing to pay it? Do we have the strength to let go of ourselves?

If the price for unity with Christ is death, are we willing to pay it?

I have seen people who treat evangelism like a game. Bringing someone to Christ is a notch on the belt of their spiritual accomplishments. Ministers pride themselves in the size of their church. Something that is all about God is being turned into something that is all about us: *our* accomplishments, *our* achievements. It's a matter of pride. Apparently, we're proud of the fact that we missed the point.

When I was in college I applied for a scholarship. When the winners were announced, I was upset. I knew one of them and thought, *Are you kidding? That guy is a self-centered jerk. Why would they pick him? He doesn't deserve that scholarship. I am better than he is; they should have picked me.* Then I realized that the real self-centered jerk was sitting in my seat, not in his. We are not here to make ourselves or our churches famous; we are here to make Jesus famous. Too often we are concerned with our own glory instead of the glory of God. We try to get people to come to our church because then our church grows. So churches battle over the saved instead of fighting for the lost. But we can't bring others the life found in Jesus until we die to ourselves.

I've also seen people for whom evangelism has become a touchy subject that they try to avoid. If we can pretend that God didn't give us this command, then we don't have to feel guilty about not doing it. We wrestle with evangelism because it can be scary. We have what Donald Whitney refers to in *Spiritual Disciplines for the Christian Life* as "evangelophobia."[2]

Rather than risk failing, we say nothing and guarantee it.

This fear of evangelism is often caused by our understanding of how important it is. So much rides on getting it right that we stress ourselves out in the moment. We believe that heaven and hell are at stake, and we find ourselves feeling overwhelmed and underprepared to deal with such responsibility. What if we fail at such an important task? Rather than risk failing, we say nothing and guarantee it.

Sometimes inadequacy gets in the way. Many Christians do not obey the command to evangelize because they feel they must have a certain amount of knowledge or they wait to have a certainty that never comes. What if the Gerasenes demoniac who had the demons cast from him by Jesus had acted that way (Mark 5:1–20)? The people in his town

Evangelism is simple: tell others what you know and let them decide what to do with it.

were terrified of him. He had been running around naked and screaming like a madman. He is certainly not the ideal candidate to proclaim the gospel. What if he had allowed his inadequacy to stop him? What if the Samaritan woman at the well had thought that way (John 4:1–26)? If anyone was going to wrestle with feelings of inadequacy, it should be this woman. She was not well thought of in the community. People would not want to hear what she had to say.

This woman knew that there was something different about Jesus, and she wanted to share that with everyone. She didn't let fear get the best of her. You might think, so what? She's in the Bible, nothing like me. Every person in Scripture has one thing in common: they are human. Not one of them is capable of doing something we are not. This lady is not great because she is in the Bible; she is in the Bible because she did something great. What she did, any one of us can do. Sometimes we make evangelism far more difficult than it needs to be. Evangelism is simple: tell others what you know and let them decide what to do with it.

In John 9 we see Jesus encountering a man who was born blind. Jesus spat in the ground to make some mud and put it on the man's eyes. Then Jesus told the man to go wash in the pool of Siloam. When this blind man did as he had been instructed, he gained his sight. Can you imagine? He had lived his whole life in darkness, having seen nothing: not hills, not the buildings of the city, not the faces of his family.

First his neighbors and then the religious leaders demanded to know how his eyes were opened, and he told them:

> "Whether he is a sinner or not, I don't know. One thing I do know. I was blind but now I see!"
>
> Then they asked him, "What did he do to you? How did he open your eyes?"

> He answered, "I have told you already and you did not listen. Why do you want to hear it again? Do you want to become his disciples, too?"
>
> Then they hurled insults at him and said, "You are this fellow's disciple! We are disciples of Moses! We know that God spoke to Moses, but as for this fellow, we don't even know where he comes from."
>
> The man answered, "Now that is remarkable! You don't know where he comes from, yet he opened my eyes. We know that God does not listen to sinners. He listens to the godly man who does his will. Nobody has ever heard of opening the eyes of a man born blind. If this man were not from God, he could do nothing." (John 9:25–33)

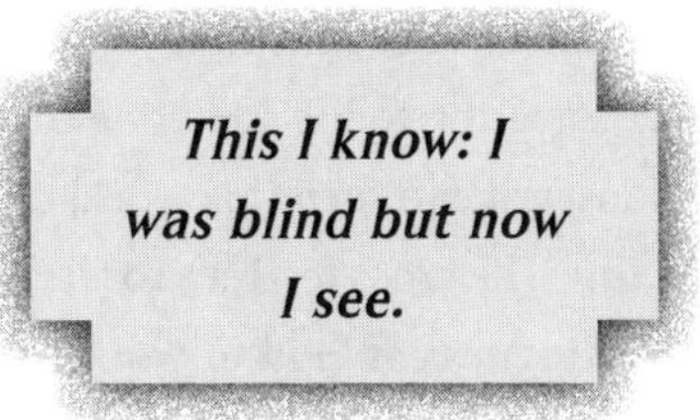

I love this guy. He's not educated. He had no Bible courses. Yet he's an incredible evangelist. Why? He simply told others what Jesus had done for him. He had been a believer for only a few minutes before he started sharing his faith. *This I know: I was blind but now I see.* Isn't that exactly what Jesus did for us? We were all blind, living in our sin, oblivious to the truth of God. And He opened our eyes. He gave us life. If this man can confidently stand before religious experts and be a witness to God after a few minutes of believing, shouldn't we be able to stand before our world as well?

So when you fear that you don't have what it takes to share the gospel with people, remember this: quit relying on your own strength. The problem with zombie strength is that it is our strength alone. Too often we rely only on what we can do and not on what God can do.

Power Failure: Connect

Look at the example Jesus set: He made sure to have plenty of time to get away and connect with God. Jesus said, I do only what I see My Father

God turned the world upside down with twelve high school dropouts from just east of nowhere.

doing (John 5:19). Even as God incarnate, He didn't try to do things on His own; His work was to glorify God in all things. To do that you have to stay connected to God through all things. There is a greater power and we need to learn how to tap into it. Too often the only strength found in our churches is human effort. Like zombie strength it may be powerful, but it is not our full potential. In combating a superhuman enemy, we need more than just our strength.

Good news: we can have it! God is willing and able to do more through us than we could ask or imagine. God turned the world upside down with twelve high school dropouts from just east of nowhere. God doesn't need your greatness, only your willingness. One person standing up with a dedication to share the love of Jesus can change everything. One person with a connection to life so strong that the raging and shaking of the world cannot loosen it can turn this world upside down. Creation testifies to the power of God. The cross testifies to the heart of God. Our commission testifies to the willingness of God to work though us. God offers us His strength, so why do we keep trying to do it on our own?

What if we learned to utilize the awesome creative power of God? Instead of bearing all the weight ourselves, what if we invited God to be a part of what we were doing? What if we called on His power, to do His work, for His kingdom? What if we learned to see our role in the kingdom of God as simply being a tool to be used? Building the kingdom of God is not about being able to do it all yourself. A hammer can't build a house alone. It is about finding your role and letting God use you in it as He sees fit. You are not the craftsman, you are the hammer. Just prepare yourself to go smash some nails.

Think about all that is required for life to exist on earth: the precise ratio of protons to electrons or the exact distance from the earth to the sun, or our planet's particular rotation and path through the solar system. If any one of these things were changed even a little, human life would not be possible.

Scientists of every kind study life on earth and the surrounding universe in which we live. Some even try to read what we observe in the creation and connect it with Scripture. One thing many scientists have noted is that the specific ingredients necessary for enabling life to exist on earth can make a striking case for an intelligent designer.[3]

Picture thousands of dials all set very specifically, like a soundboard. At the atomic level, the statistical probability of just one dial being tuned by chance to achieve the necessary ratio of electron to proton mass to enable life on earth to exist is 1 in 10 to the 37th power (10^{37} = one followed by 37 zeros). If the universe were larger or smaller, chemical bonding would be insufficient for life chemistry.[4] That's just one dial. At the astrophysical level, the statistical probability of another one of those dials being tuned by chance to reconcile the amount of matter density in the universe with the amount of "stuff" out there called dark energy density required to account for the flat universe we observe today is at least 1 in 10 to the 120th power (10^{120} = one followed by 120 zeros).[5] The flatness of our universe is due to a certain "springiness" to space, presumably this dark energy stuff functioning as a cosmological constant that somehow causes the universe to expand at a faster rate the more it expands.[6] Slightly amazed yet or just bewildered? The fine-tuning parameters for the universe are equally amazing in this view of things. If the universe were smaller, galaxies would not form because the universe would expand too quickly to form solar-type stars necessary to sustain life. If the universe were larger, galaxies or galaxy clusters would be too dense for life; black holes and neutron stars would dominate and the universe would collapse before a site suitable for life could form.[7] And that "site suitable for life" is the planet God created for us to live on: "In the beginning God created the heavens and the earth" (Gen. 1:1). Each of these thousands of different dials is tuned perfectly to enable human life on earth. If just one of those dials shifted ever so slightly, it would destroy the possibility for human existence altogether.

Now imagine this: cover the entire North American continent with dimes. North America is approximately 9,450,000 square miles.[8] Now find one hundred billion additional continents of the same size and cover them in dimes. Done? Good. Then add layers of dimes all the way up to the moon,

God is awesome, the universe is not an accident, and God is really detailed with His creation.

about 239,000 miles high. Now paint one dime blue and randomly toss that one blue dime into the pile of dimes. Blindfold a friend and have him pick one dime, then put that dime back. (Nope, hang on, we're not done yet.) Mix them all up and have him pick another. The odds he will pick out the blue dime one hundred times in a row would actually be greater than the odds of just one of these dials being tuned in such a way as to enable the existence of human life.[9] If you feel like you can't make heads or tails of this, here's the point not to miss: God is awesome, the universe is not an accident, and God is really detailed with His creation.

Let's look at it differently. A few years ago I had the opportunity to go to Rome. While we were there, one of the places we visited was St. Peter's Basilica, said to be the resting place of St. Peter himself, one of Jesus' twelve disciples. The entire interior of this beautiful building is made of gold and marble. It is a truly wonderful thing to see.

What impressed me more than the Basilica itself was the courtyard. (It's called "the square" even though it's really more of a circle.) This incredible courtyard contains 284 columns that run four rows deep, two on either side. Each of these columns stands around forty-three feet tall and about ten feet wide. The exterior of the Basilica is built symmetrically, so that from a single spot an entire half-circle of these enormous columns are hidden.

I remember just standing there in awe considering how brilliant the architect who designed this had to be. When you look at a beautiful painting, you realize that an artist must have painted it. When you look at a great computer, you appreciate the efforts of a Steven Jobs. So what do we think of when we see the magnificent world around us?

A few weeks ago I heard about these orioles in Africa that build nests that look like purses hanging down from trees. There is another kind of bird called the cowbird. These birds come in and leave their eggs in oriel nests.

Cowbirds are the deadbeats of the animal kingdom. They drop their kids off to be raised by someone else.

Baby orioles face a danger: botflies can kill baby orioles. If the mother oriel builds her nest near a beehive, she knows the bees will prevent botflies, and so she throws out the cowbird egg before it hatches. If, however, the nest is in a tree with no bees nearby, the mother bird will raise the cowbird because the cowbird baby will eat the botflies off of the oriole babies.[10] How do these orioles instinctively know to do that?

Or consider the honeybee. When a bee finds pollen or nectar, it goes back to the hive and it stands pointing in the direction of the food source. Then it does a dance (maybe to R. Kelly's "I Believe I Can Fly"), and while the bee dances, the other bees count how many times it spins around and that tells them how far away the food is. Bees have rhythm with a purpose. Where did these bees learn to do that?

I think about the world around us, with its many different animals and creatures both great and small. Each one is unique in its own way. God didn't just make the world function; He made it beautiful. God made the waters of the oceans softly reflect the light of the sun. God changed the color of the skies for sunset and sunrise so that every day would begin and end with something beautiful. I think about things like the aurora borealis with its many colors dancing through the nights of the northern skies. I think about the God who has made all of this with a few words, and you know what comes to my mind? I think that God is bored.

I think that God is bored.

I think that God is bored with the petty faith of our American churches. When was the last time we did something that would require God to act? When was the last time our churches stepped out in faith to do something so big, we would need God to be a part of it? I am not saying we haven't done anything. We have accomplished *some* great things, but for a nation of "Christian" people and two hundred years of working at it, you would think we would have accomplished a lot more.

I imagine God sitting up in heaven just waiting from someone to do something that would require Him to be involved. He's like a dad in a pool, trying to encourage his child to jump in. God has all this power and creativity, and what is His church doing that would even allow Him to use it? What if we changed that? What if we stopped being another religious institution? What if we put religion to death and became a people who dared to step out in faith so much so that we challenged God to act in our lives? I think God would rather we fail miserably with our hearts in the right place than for us to succeed masterfully by our own strength. What if we threw out all the ideas of nominal growth or incremental growth? So what if we stopped playing safe and dared to do something huge?

Superhuman Strength

It all starts with one church. One group being willing to step out in faith and to be the spark that lights the world on fire. What if we prayed something so big that we could never do it? What if we pursued something so great that we could never hope to achieve it on our own? What if we had a vision so big that only God could get credit for it if we pulled it off?

We have access to this awesome creative power, and to be honest we are wasting it. Sure we pray for things like healing for Aunt Judy and health for Grandpa Joe, but God's power is for more than just the occasional healing of sick relatives.

God has challenged us to do something so big that we can never do it on our own. That is the point. God doesn't want to do it Himself. He doesn't want us to do it ourselves. There is a reason Matthew 28 isn't called the Great Mission but the Great Co[-]mission: God wants to do this together.

My prayer is that we would be transformed from religious people to spiritual people. I think God is bored with our trivial acts of worship because He is not part of the process. It is time for us to stop being a church in the religious sense and start being a connecting point to Jesus. We need to stop being the church we have made and start being the church we were made to be. God is not bored with the church, He's just bored with what we've done with it.

We need to get out into the world and make a difference. The church should impact this world. Our views and our thoughts should change things. You might think that's too big a task for my little church. Yes it is. That is the point. This task is too big for any of us. So when we try to accomplish it, we have to make God the primary driving force. Let's forget about everything we have done in our past. Let's forget the mistakes and start over. We need to build off a foundation that relies on God. Here's what that looks like: love. You want to know what is so big that we cannot hope to do it without God? Love. You want to know what challenge we could give that would require God to act? Love. You want to know what will impact this world for Jesus? Love. I think that God is bored because we are not loving to our full potential. Love gets God excited.

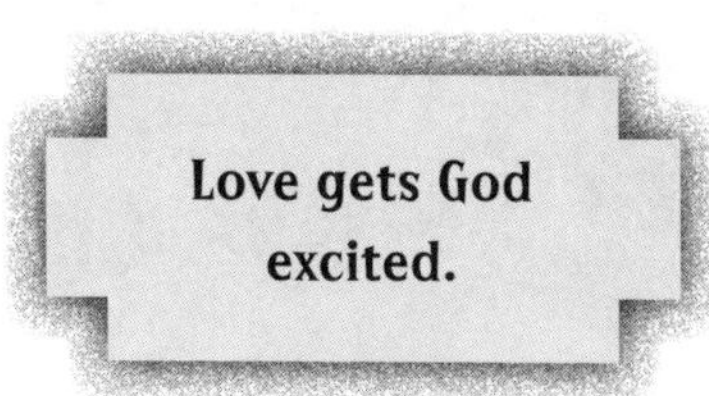

God gets excited about love. When we love we are fulfilling the original purpose of our creation. We need to go out into the world and to love people like Jesus loved them. For too long we have been content inside our four nice walls, warming our slightly less than comfortable pews.

The issues that face the world are not new, neither is our awareness of them. We have sat idly by while children starved, people died of curable diseases, and many lived in extreme poverty. It is not that we have done nothing, but we have not done enough. We live in a world we know needs Jesus.

What are we going to do about it? Will we continue to spectate or will we start over, forget about practicalities, and do something so big that God would step in to be a part of it? I am tired of doing the Christian thing, of living the routine and the ritual. If you are tired of that too, then it's time to do something about it. It's time to wake up and bring life back to the church. Our Zombie churches would quickly be cured if every Christian would individually love God with the entirety of their mind, heart, soul, and strength.

Chapter Nine

THE DISEASE SPREADS

Although zombie movies offer different theories as to why the dead return to life (or at least to being undead), on the silver screen it is a universal truth that zombiism is infectious. When a living person either gets bitten by a zombie, comes in contact with the blood of a zombie, or dies, he or she begins to transform into one. In the film *I Am Legend* (2007),[1] the zombie creatures are a result of a quickly spreading virus that turns men into monsters. Robert Neville is a scientist who for some reason is immune to the virus, and he is driven to find a way to reverse the disease and bring life back to the world.

There are zombies among us. They show up to the services, sit in the chairs, sing the songs, even listen to the sermons. While the percentage of zombies may vary from church to church, no churches are without their share of the undead. Zombiism is a disease that slowly drains life from the church. It pulls us from a closer relationship with God into mindless religious practice in which there is no life. Those who have been infected with this disease are determined to infect others, and no one is completely immune.

I am asthmatic. My lungs react to things that are not toxins as if they are and close up when I do not take proper medicine. Pets, dust, grass, pollens, and exercise can all set off my condition at any time. Asthma, left untreated, can be fatal. There is no cure for asthma, but there is treatment. Medicine prevents me from having asthma attacks or helps calm them down if I do. The same is true with zombiism, there is no cure—in this fallen world—but there is a treatment. The answer is not found in doing something once but in an antidote that we must continually keep with us. That antidote can prevent us from having zombie outbreaks by keeping our hearts in tune with the heart of God.

The Bible doesn't talk about zombies per se, and yet Jesus used a similar analogy in talking about the sheep and the goats. During Bible times, it would have been common for several flocks of sheep and goats to come together for the night. Sometimes they even grazed together. But while these two kinds of animals look similar, there is a great difference in their value. Zombie churches might look similar to churches with life, but there is a great difference in their value. While the distinction may not always be obvious to us now, when Jesus returns the distinction will be very clear.

Sheep and Goats

Distinguishing the sheep from the goats is very important. Sheep are more valuable to the shepherd because their wool can be used to make all sorts of things. Goats also have fur, but it is not nearly as valuable. Matthew 25 shows how to distinguish one from the other: those who belong to Jesus will behave in a certain way, while those who do not . . . won't.

> When the Son of Man comes in his glory . . . all the nations will be gathered before him, and he will separate the people one from another as a shepherd separates the sheep from the goats. He will put the sheep on his right and the goats on his left.
>
> Then the King will say to those on his right, "Come, you who are blessed by my Father; take your inheritance, the kingdom prepared for you since the creation of the world. For I was

> hungry and you gave me something to eat, I was thirsty and you gave me something to drink, I was a stranger and you invited me in, I needed clothes and you clothed me, I was sick and you looked after me, I was in prison and you came to visit me."
>
> Then the righteous will answer him, "Lord, when did we see you hungry and feed you, or thirsty and give you something to drink? When did we see you a stranger and invite you in, or needing clothes and clothe you? When did we see you sick or in prison and go to visit you?"
>
> The King will reply, "I tell you the truth, whatever you did for one of the least of these brothers of mine, you did for me."
>
> Then he will say to those on his left, "Depart from me, you who are cursed, into the eternal fire prepared for the devil and his angels. For I was hungry and you gave me nothing to eat, I was thirsty and you gave me nothing to drink, I was a stranger and you did not invite me in, I needed clothes and you did not clothe me, I was sick and in prison and you did not look after me."
>
> They also will answer, "Lord, when did we see you hungry or thirsty or a stranger or needing clothes or sick or in prison, and did not help you?"
>
> He will reply, "I tell you the truth, whatever you did not do for one of the least of these, you did not do for me."
>
> Then they will go away to eternal punishment, but the righteous to eternal life. (Matt. 25:31–46)

You see, belonging to Jesus does not come from talking about Him but from living like Him. We care for the poor because we love Jesus, and Jesus loves the poor. We feed the hungry because, having experienced the love of Jesus, we want to share His love with them by meeting their needs. (We must remember that we do not do these things to *earn* our salvation.) When we love Jesus it affects what we do.

If you struggle with this, especially with just knowing who you are as a part of God's flock, then pray: "God help me see people the way that You do. Help me love them the way that You do." God does not ask you to be like Jesus and then leave you alone to figure out what that means. God wants to help you, to lead you each step of the way. If you're not sure that you are on the right path, then there is probably a problem. Ask God where He is leading you. Ask Him to let you see the world through His eyes so you can follow Him more genuinely. Aligning yourself with God—or syncing yourself, for you tech-savvy iPod users—is really the best way to become a sheep instead of a goat.

Not meant to be an exhaustive list, this passage in Matthew highlights six deeds that are characteristic of Jesus' followers—actions that meet the basic needs of every person for food, clothing, shelter, and acceptance.

Notice that the sheep are shocked at the response they get from the king. They hadn't done these things to earn something; they did them because, having experienced the love of God, they couldn't stop themselves from sharing God's love with others. When Jesus meets your needs, naturally you want to respond by helping meet the needs of others. The sheep are shocked that the king would even recognize what they did, because they don't remember doing anything worth recognizing.

Scripture teaches not a doctrine of good works . . . but an outworking of one's doctrine.

The goats on the other hand are sent to hell. Not necessarily because they did evil things but because they neglected good things. Their lack of action betrays their lack of commitment to the Son of God. They may have "paid their dues" so to speak, but they didn't really have that relationship with Him. Scripture teaches not a doctrine of good works . . . but an outworking of one's doctrine. The danger of Zombie churches is that they are all about going through the motions of religious behavior, but in the process they are neglecting the people that God loves.

The goats are surprised because they had neglected a real commitment to a relationship with Jesus and felt their hollow religious practices were enough. So when they are punished, they say: "Wait a minute! We know the rules, we kept them. We don't drink, don't smoke, don't do drugs, we don't have sex outside of marriage, we don't dance, or run at church. Why are you punishing us?" Jesus says: "You may not have done anything wrong, but you didn't do anything right either. You had an opportunity to show your love for Me by caring for those who needed you, and you didn't. I am love and because you did not love, you are not a part of Me."

Perhaps it is time for another prayer. "God, show me how I look to You. Am I where You want me to be? If not, how do I get there?"

The church has been given a great task of caring for the lost and the hurting people of this world. We are commissioned to feed the hungry, to care for the sick, and to visit the lonely. In too many cases, the church isn't doing that, but we can't claim that we didn't know we were supposed to. Jesus makes His expectations very clear: His people will take care of the basic needs of humanity. Most of what I want to do in this chapter is just create an awareness of the disease and how widespread Zombiism really is. Evidence of the disease is seen in our comfortable homes, luxury cars, extravagant clothes and jewelry, lavish entertainments, and expensive hobbies. We can't afford to ignore this; the stakes for eternity both for ourselves and for the lost are too high.

The Chasm

Jesus calls His followers to tend to the basic needs of others. Rather than sacrificing personal comforts for the good of those in need, we have turned our lives into little storehouses, accumulating all this stuff we don't need while outside our safe walls there are people who do not have walls at all, not because they chose it but because they live in a world that is so poor, they never got a choice. Paul really strikes at this issue in his second letter to the Corinthians:

> Our desire is not that others might be relieved while you are hard pressed, but that there might be equality. At the present time your plenty will supply what they need, so that in turn

> their plenty will supply what you need. Then there will be equality, as it is written: "He who gathered much did not have too much, and he who gathered little did not have too little." (2 Cor. 8:13–15)

The problems of the world especially when it comes to salvation are not our responsibility. It's not our job to save the world. That's what God does. This is not an obligation but an invitation. We are invited by God to be a part of His work in the world. If we will partner with Him, we have the hope of a more perfect world. We have an opportunity to help turn the world into a place where everyone has enough. Is there a better portrait of a godly community than this? What if we did this maybe just within the church community? What if no one in the church ever had too little? Don't you think that outsiders would naturally be drawn to a community like that?

It's not our job to save the world. That's what God does.

Look at the opportunity we have in this world to use our excess for the benefit of those in need. According to a census taken by the United Nations, based on 1997 reports on spending, Americans spend around $8 billion per year on cosmetics. The price of beauty in the United States alone *exceeds* the estimated additional annual cost of providing basic education for all by $2 billion. For all those animal lovers out there, the amount spent on pet food in the United States and Europe combined is $17 billion annually, but it would cost only $13 billion annually to offer basic health and nutrition to all members of developing countries. Seems our pets are better off than children in some countries. For that extra $13 billion, we could feed all the starving children we see on commercials. It would be rather easy to do considering we spend over ten times that on alcohol.[2] Hey, maybe if we invested in helping others in need, we wouldn't need to spend so much on filling that void in our lives with booze. Just a thought.

Certainly seeing these numbers reveals the chasm that exists between the haves and the have-nots. We spend more on perfumes and pet food than it would take to supply clean water and food to all developing countries, and those numbers are from over a decade ago. Do you think our fatal attraction to consumerism in America has shrunk or grown since then? Jesus expects His followers to take care of the basic needs of others: food, clothing, shelter, and acceptance. So how are we doing in those areas?

The Basics

Water is one of the simplest and most basic needs in life and also one that we take for granted every day. We have ready access to clean water, and yet we get upset if the clean water tastes a little funny or if it takes a moment to start flowing. I wonder if just realizing the needs of the world might change our perspective a little bit.

When I was in Uganda, I taught a class on the life of Christ. We were in John 4, talking about the woman at the well, and I was going into the history of how this woman had to travel a quarter mile from her village to get to Jacob's well. Realizing that some of my students were from rural areas, I stopped and asked if any of them had to travel to get to clean water. A few of them raised their hands. I asked how far they had to go, and I learned that one of my students had to travel four miles every day just to get to clean water. They didn't need my history lesson; they already understood the situation of the woman at the well because they lived it and then some. Most of them had never been to a place where water was supplied through faucets. I have not thought of water the same way since.

We don't really understand hunger if we have never looked it in the eyes. Sure, we see TV commercials of children who have stomachs bloated from hunger, but most of us haven't looked into those children's eyes in person as we took a bite of a big cheeseburger and said, "I'm sorry, but I just don't have anything to give you."

Approximately 1.2 billion people suffer from hunger and some 2 to 3.5 billion people have a deficiency of vitamins and minerals because they can't get the right foods to eat. Yet at the same time, 1.2 billion people suffer from obesity.[3] The Institute for Food and Development Policy has said:

> The food crisis appeared to explode overnight, reinforcing fears that there are just too many people in the world. But according to the FAO [the United Nations Food and Agriculture Organization], with record grain harvests in 2007, there is more than enough food in the world to feed everyone—at least 1.5 times current demand. In fact, over the last 20 years, food production has risen steadily at over 2.0% a year, while the rate of population growth has dropped to 1.14% a year. Population is not outstripping food supply. "We're seeing more people hungry and at greater numbers than before," says World Hunger Program's executive director Josette Sheeran, "There is food on the shelves but people are priced out of the market."[4]

Just looking at this unequal distribution of wealth—or as we like to call it, "The American Dream"—should open our eyes. How did we neglect to consider that the obscene wealth of one would mean the radical poverty of one hundred? The United Nations' development program reported that "for the first time in human history, the amount of overweight people rivals the number of underweight people." While billions are not getting the necessary nutrients they need, obesity cost the United States $118 billion in the late 1990s.[5]

Do you see the problem? We realize that it is a bad thing to have too little. What we don't often stop to consider is that it is just as bad to have too much. Surrounded by excess, we have forgotten what life is about. The American Dream tells us that happiness comes from owning everything you want . . . and more, but the people who get there aren't happy. The dream turns into a nightmare when we become consumed by the surplus of our lives.

The dream turns into a nightmare when we become consumed by the surplus of our lives.

Zombies are not healthy creatures—they ravenously consume people without any thought of moderation. A healthy life requires balance. It means not having too little but at the same time not having too much.

An article from Fox News featured a woman who currently weighs over six hundred pounds and has set a goal to weigh one thousand. She wants to weigh half a ton. Well, why not? As she says, she's not hurting anyone by eating and people love watching her eat.[6] Do you find this appalling? If you're tempted to judge her harshly, be careful. All this woman is doing is hoarding the excess. Some of us do that with electronics, with sports, with cars.

When we hoard something—anything—we are believing the lie that those things are necessary for our happiness. We use things to try to satisfy a void in our lives. It is one thing for the world to buy into these lies. Why do we believe them in the church? Why isn't the love of Jesus enough for us? Why do we need all these possessions to makes us feel important or significant?

Thank God that He isn't a communist.

God has given us such a wonderful opportunity. Some people do not have enough. Some people have too much. So here is the solution: those who have in excess should share. If you have something you don't need, just pray that God will put you in contact with someone in need, so you can rid yourself of the excess while meeting another's need. It's a perfect system. You get to be blessed by sharing love in a practical way, and that person in need gets to be blessed by receiving God's provision through you. What a wonderful opportunity! Thank God that He isn't a communist. He has given more to some so they can help others. He has blessed us so that we can experience His love by sharing what He has given. In so doing we become the vessel for God to distribute His love to the world. God gives you what He does so you can use it.

Make a Difference

Look back at these issues and then at Matthew 25. If those who are followers of Jesus are known for what they do, then do we look like Jesus? The church today has access to more resources and readily available funding than it ever has in history. Yet how much effort have we made to clothe the naked, take care of the sick, feed the hungry, and give rest to the weary?

How will history remember us? The church in Acts 2 was unified and had everything in common. The church of the second and third centuries endured through persecution. We remember the early church of America in its establishment of religious freedom. What will be said about our churches in the years to come? That we were a church of plenty living in a land of opportunities that we never took? That we built impressive buildings with multifunctional seating and to-die-for sound systems? Will we be remembered as the church that carried out the Great Commission? Or the church that was Gloriously Comfortable?

The American church is complacent. We sit back and do nothing while the least of these starve to death or are sold as slaves and sexually exploited. We have hidden ourselves within the four walls of the church and ignored the cries of the world around us.

A church that sees the needs of the world and does nothing is a Zombie church. A Zombie church is not necessarily falling apart and about to close its doors; it can be filled with people every Sunday. A Zombie church is a church that neglects the people that Jesus loves. A Zombie church is a church that has lost sight of its purpose and identity.

But before getting discouraged, consider this: in Matthew 14 there is an enormous crowd of people listening to Jesus teach. He teaches all day and they get hungry. All Jesus has to work with is a little boy's sack lunch. Yet through the power of God, everyone in the crowd ate and had their fill *and* the disciples gathered up more food than they had started with. We are talking about upwards of ten to fifteen thousand people, and Jesus feeds them with a Snackable. Jesus doesn't need us to be able to meet the need—He wants us to be willing to help. Jesus can handle the multiplication, but we need to bring Him our lunch boxes.

God is bigger than all the hunger issues of the world; He has already proved that. God can take care of all of this. So, you might ask, why doesn't He? The church is God's redemptive agent in the world. If God did it all for us, we would have no purpose. God does not desire to do the work *for* us but *with* us.

Here is the cure: you are not responsible for fixing all the things that are wrong in the world. But you should love the person whom God puts in front of you each day. If you can commit to doing that, God can change the world through you. If you try to do this without God, you fail. If you don't try to do this at all, you fail.

The world around us has a need. The American church has been blessed with enough extra to help meet that need. We can be the love of Jesus to someone by sharing with them and accommodating their needs. Love will motivate us to act on behalf of others. We are invited to be conduits of God's loving provision, His living water, to the world. Love does not worry about what it must sacrifice. It cares too much about the needs that sacrifice can meet. Love would rather give away everything than do nothing. We cannot sit back and do nothing about the needs of the world. God blesses us so that we can turn around and bless others.

The love of God doesn't, won't, can't run out.

Ultimately, I think we want to share the love we have, but we are afraid that if we give it away, there won't be any more for us. But when we hold onto what we have, we prevent ourselves from being able to receive more. Cup your hands—how much can they hold? Now open your hands and imagine water pouring onto them and out of them, spilling everywhere. When we hold onto what we have, we effectively limit our ability to be blessed by God. But when we open our hands, He can just keep on pouring. The love of God doesn't, won't, can't run out. It is a stream of living water that never runs dry. The great thing about it, unlike the water company, is that God doesn't penalize you for usage: on the contrary, He rewards you for it.

Chapter Ten

ZOMBIE COMMUNITY

Zombieland (2009)[1] is a little lighter take on the typical zombie movie. The main character is a teenage loner. He avoided social contact with people when they were alive, and yet as the world turns to zombies, he finds himself getting lonely. At the end of the movie, he reflects on the events that have transpired and the friends he has made, and he comes to a wonderful realization: without relationships with other people, we are all just zombies. Rarely do I expect to be impressed with the depth of anything said in a zombie movie, so that really surprised me. We are meant to be connected. Life, and especially the true life found in Christ, is not something you can do on your own.

These are churches where God might be taught, but He is not attending.

The church has become something it was never intended to be and entire generations don't know any better. The only church some people have ever known is the commercialized, culturally infected, Zombie church that reigns throughout our country. These are churches that fight over power and control. These are churches where people are split into groups that bicker and argue. These are churches where God might be taught, but He is not attending. In some, He is not even welcome.

The mass exodus from organized religion and traditional church is happening today for a reason. The church is offering a "product" that it is failing to deliver: *life*. It is making promises that it doesn't keep and people are getting tired of it. They are weary of showing up at the doors of the church looking for answers and leaving with a sense of disappointment and dissatisfaction.

After the Lights Go Out

For anyone who is not of the old-school, traditional mind-set, church is losing its appeal. It reminds me of the seven churches of Revelation 2 and 3. Jesus threatens a few of them that if they do not shape up, He will come and take away their lampstand. I wonder if that isn't what's happened in some of our churches. Perhaps the lampstand, the fire of God, is gone, and so we are clinging to the rituals that we remember from when God was there last. Instead of repenting and turning back to God, we just hold onto symbols and rituals from when God was with us. How often do we hear people in the church talking about the glory days when the church was alive?

Church is becoming a boring tradition. Even when we crank up the music, it still lacks a certain luster. It has become dry and mundane. So people are starting to look in other places for what the church should be giving them. We are all looking for life. If the church doesn't have it, we move on to something else.

The problem is when the real community has less actual community than the counterfeits.

Part of the reason the world does not realize its need for the community of the church is because there are so many readily available counterfeits. These counterfeits take away the symptoms without giving people what they need. Places like Starbucks are so effective at creating an easily accessible community that people don't realize their need for the community of Christ.

If you don't know what real community looks like, you can't tell the fakes from the real. The problem is when the real community has less actual community than the counterfeits. It would be like if there was so much counterfeit money circulating that we started thinking that *real* money was counterfeit because it was different than what we were used to.

A friend told me about a conversation she was having with her dad. He was an old-school fire-and-brimstone preacher. Unfortunately, he used the Word of God to give himself power over others. Over dinner this guy was talking to his daughter about the laws of God. Her boyfriend, who was not a Christian, started to protest. The reason he is not a Christian is that he had known too many Christians. She started telling her dad that what we needed was to show the love of Jesus. (This made me very happy since it was straight from our current sermon series at the time. Few things are as rewarding to a preacher as knowing that something he said got through.) Her dad responded, "Yeah, but we have to look at these seventy laws given by God to the nation of Israel. When we understand those, we have to analyze the lives of the disciples and study the prophets and the law so we can know how to live the Christian life."

We have turned the church into a synagogue, and its leaders are becoming modern-day Pharisees.

Oh, is that all? All we have to do is study and memorize every nuance of the law in the Old Testament and then build life principles from the disciples, and then we can be Christians?

Studying the law has value, but Jesus sums up the whole law in two commands: love God and love people. Zombie churches make Christianity really complicated. It becomes an incredibly detailed list of dos and don'ts. No wonder people are looking for more. No wonder they are tired of church. We have turned the church into a synagogue, and its leaders are becoming modern-day Pharisees.

It is not my intent in any way to downplay the importance of holiness in our lives. But holiness is far from the result you get when leaders take what should be a beautiful desire in the heart of every Christian and turn it into a weapon used to smack people over the head. And all the worse when people who brag as if they have a direct line from God live contrary to the most important law He gave us: love.

I am sure we have all had those days where we wake up on a Sunday morning and just want to stay home. After a long week without enough sleep, it can be tempting to just snooze through church. Haven't you ever wondered about how your church attendance relates to your spiritual life?

You don't have to go to church to be a Christian any more than a fish has to be in water to be a fish.

For a long time the church answered this question badly. They bullied and guilt-tripped people into being there every week and created this idea that your relationship with God is essentially based on your church attendance. Not only then was there a conception that if you attended church, you would be saved but also, in some people's eyes, that was *all* you needed to do to be saved. People react like a pendulum: when things push to far one way, they react by pushing back too far the other way. So in reaction to this incorrect focus on church attendance, people have begun rebelling against organized religion in general, and regular church attendance in particular.

The church is designed to be radically inclusive. When the church is alive it is magnetic, even irresistible. The community that we have is one that people naturally long for. The church is a community built with support, encouragement, friendship, dedication, service, and love. The world offers substitutes, but when the church does what it was designed to do, nothing in the world can compare to the quality of what we offer. So why aren't more people drawn to it? The church is uniquely equipped to meet humanity's need for community, both now and for eternity, by bringing people to Jesus. So why are so many saying, "I don't like church"? It's like we long for the community of God in heaven while despising the community of God on earth. I hear people say this all the time: "You don't have to go to church to be a Christian." They're right. You don't have to go to church to be a Christian any more than a fish has to be in water to be a fish. A fish is still a fish out of water; it just won't live long.

I understand the church has its problems. Here is where it all comes together for me: the church is not perfect because we are a part of it. The church is a place where imperfect people imperfectly follow imperfect leaders who lead in imperfect ways. All human activity within the church is imperfect. I am imperfect, you are imperfect, and so it's only natural that the church is flawed. The only way for the church to be perfect is for us to stop being a part of it, but then it wouldn't be the church.

Antisocial

There are Zombie churches, and many of us have been burned by them. But that's not an acceptable reason to walk away from the church altogether. To do so is to disobey the Word of God. Speaking for God the Father, Jesus says, "If you love me, you will obey what I command" and "He who does not love me will not obey my teaching" (John 14:15, 24). And God commands us not to forsake the church.

The book in the Bible called Hebrews is written to a group of people not all that different from us. Apparently, there were people who had begun to slip away from their relationship with the church and were forsaking the community. So the author challenged them and urged them to stay the course:

> Let us not give up meeting together, as some are in the habit of doing, but let us encourage one another—and all the more as you see the Day approaching. (Heb. 10:25)

It is easy to view Christianity as just another religion asking for you to accept and to attend. Indeed this seems to be the problem the Hebrews were dealing with in the early church. They apparently had Christians who were living without the supporting community of the church because they had failed to understand its proper significance and role in their lives. Some had begun to neglect their connection to the community, and this is a dangerous road to walk down. The passage in Hebrews continues:

> If we deliberately keep on sinning after we have received the knowledge of the truth, no sacrifice for sins is left, but only a fearful expectation of judgment and of raging fire that will consume the enemies of God. Anyone who rejected the law of Moses died without mercy on the testimony of two or three witnesses. How much more severely do you think a man deserves to be punished who has trampled the Son of God under foot, who has treated as an unholy thing the blood of the covenant that sanctified him, and who has insulted the Spirit of grace? (Heb. 10:26–29)

When we neglect our relationship with the church, we often fall into the sins of our past. When we make this choice and keep on sinning, we are spitting in Jesus' face and insulting the sacrifice He made for us. When we fail to commit ourselves to the community of the church, we are disobeying God's command. Tolerating disobedience is a slippery slope. I have watched people step away from the church because they were burned or burnt out. From what I've seen, the result has never been an improvement in their relationship with God. They typically just seem to slowly slide into sin. Losing our connection to the community of God's people can damage our connection to God Himself as God will often use His people to speak to us. Without godly people invested in our lives, we don't have examples to follow or people to hold us accountable. This can result in a full-out rejection of God's grace and ultimately can lead to our own destruction. We need to make sure we stay connected with the church, for when we fail to do so, we bring trouble on ourselves. I am not saying our church attendance is a salvational issue, but it is a significant one.

It may seem better to stay at home and have personal time with God rather than to go to another lifeless church service. Believe me, I understand how unsatisfying a church that does not offer life can be. But look at it this way: Let's say that, as someone who sees the lack of life in the church, your role in the body is to be the nervous system. Pain is the body's warning system that something is wrong. If the warning sensors stay home, then how will the church ever realize there is a problem? So, one reason to remain in the church is for the sake of the church as a whole.

There is a real danger that comes when we neglect meeting together. When we fail to be a regular part of the church or get in the habit of attending but not building real relationships, we are basically putting ourselves outside of the church. Have you ever noticed that when a lion is stalking a herd of gazelle, the one he goes after is usually the one that breaks away from the herd? When we neglect our relationship with the church, we make ourselves more vulnerable to sin. So, a second reason you should remain in the church is to protect yourself from sin.

When we fail to invest ourselves in the church, we disqualify ourselves from many of the blessings God may seek to give us. I am reminded of this story about a man who had missed church for a number of weeks. The minister had often called him and asked where he was, but the man kept putting the minister off. Finally, one cold wintery day the minister stopped by for a visit. The man welcomed the preacher, sat with him in front of the fireplace, and then tried to engage him in conversation, but the minister didn't seem interested in conversation. The minister had walked over to the fireplace, pulled one of the logs away from the flame, and then sat down again. They sat there in silence for a while just watching the fire. As they watched, the log that sat off by itself began to smolder and then its fire went out. The preacher and the man sat for a long time looking into the fireplace. Finally the man broke the silence: "OK, I'll be at church next Sunday."

This demonstrates both points. By itself, the log could not sustain fire. It is difficult enough to stay on course in this life when we help support each other. When we go off on our own, drifting is almost a guarantee. It doesn't take long for that drifting to get us off course and for us to become truly lost. And without that log, the whole fire did not burn as brightly, as hotly, or as long. Not only do you need church for your personal growth and relationship with God, but the church also needs you. God has uniquely gifted each of us to play an important role in His kingdom and community. Without you the rest of the church suffers from lack of resources.

In a godless world, the church is our most tangible and personal connection with God. When the fullness of God's Spirit is described in Scripture, it is plural. The Spirit does not fully rest on us as individuals but on us as the church; it is only when God's people meet together in community that the fullness of His Spirit and His gifts can be received. The Lord's Supper or communion is one of those together times (1 Cor. 10:16–17). Whenever we meet as a church and use the various gifts of the Spirit that Christ gives us to serve and help one another, we receive that fullness of God's grace anew (Rom. 12:4–5; 1 Cor. 12:12–20). That, however, also requires unity, which comes from His people building relationships with one another (Eph. 4:3–16).

We're in this together. We are joined by a common hope, purpose, joy, life, and Savior. We have been called to the same mission; we have the same goals and the same reason for accomplishing them. For the God who gives us all the same eternal life calls us to join together. We invest in each other because we are called by the same God to do the same work and to do it together.

If we are not faithful with the church, why should God entrust us with more? How often do we seek God's will in our lives? Ever feel like you get the answer? Often God does not give us the specifics until we get the general idea right. If we are not faithful with the big picture, why should God entrust us with the details? Notice that Jesus did not send the disciples out until He had trained them. He did not give them the commission and His specific purpose for their lives until they had gotten the first things right. If you want to know what God's will is in your life, then you need to get the general things down first. One of the more important general investments we make in our lives is in the community of the church. This is often the place where people will hear or find God's specific call in their lives.

Can you be a Christian without going to church? The very asking of the question is missing the point. A true Christian will desire to go to church. Having a real relationship with God creates in us an innate desire to be with His people. When we feel the touch of God on our lives and realize Jesus' sacrifice for our sins and the price He paid for us, we naturally respond by wanting to be around others who have experienced that same joy. We seek to find those who can help guide us and show us how to grow closer to Jesus in response to His love. We naturally desire . . . *more.* Genuine Christians will rarely find themselves passing on opportunities to spend time with the people of God. It just seems to go against their nature.

The church is like a gas station: it's not the destination, but it provides you with the resources to get there.

The church is a gift and we should treasure it. More importantly, we should *be* it. The church cannot really be the church until we engage in community with each other and invest in the world around us. We gather together so that together we can find the strength to go out and show the world the love of God. Don't be confused—church isn't what you are supposed to *do*; church is what gives you the *strength* to do what you need to do. The church is like a gas station: it's not the destination, but it provides you with the resources to get there. Our gathering together prepares us to be what God intends us to be—a dynamic community that turns the world upside down by sharing the love and life of Jesus with others.

Now this is the importance of church. It is not, however, what should motivate us to be a part of it. The problem is not in going to church or not going to church—that's just the stem of the problem, not the root. We should not go to church because it is an obligation. We should not go because it makes God love us more or earns our salvation. We should go to church because we are stronger together. Jesus loves us and He gave us the church for a reason. As iron sharpens iron, we can help each other be better. When we stand together, we can stand; when we separate, the enemy can tear us apart. The church is the theater in which God chooses to display

His awesome glory.[2] Leaving the church is like watching the previews and leaving before the main feature. If you leave the church, you are missing the main feature.

The Irresistible Church

There is something irresistible about a living church. It is a place where things are how they should be. Nothing in the world can offer the unconditional love that can be found in the church. What will bring life back to our churches is learning to view them differently. Going to church is not an obligation. It is not what makes God love you. Going to church is the way you connect with God through His community on earth and better learn how to follow Him.

We need to stop church-shopping, looking for the best deals on grace and Jesus at the church with the best customer service. The church that becomes a Zombie church does so because we turn it into one. In order for life to exist in the church community, we have to stop fighting over who gets their needs met and start working at meeting the needs of others. If we want to bring life back to the church, we have to become a selfless community.

There are certain controversial issues that every Christian generation must deal with. When the church was still very young, one of the primary issues pertained to food. The Jews were God's chosen people under the old covenant. But now a new covenant had come. The new church wrestled with the question of whether you had to be a Jew—and follow all the laws—before you could become a Christian. An honest and reasonable question.

In Jewish society, food laws were of the utmost importance. What you ate and who you ate with was a matter of purity. If you were to look at rabbinic tradition, you would find 341 case rulings or laws for the Pharisees to uphold. Of those rulings, no less than 229 pertain to table fellowship.[3] For a Jew to eat with a Gentile would mean sacrificing one of the primary things that set them apart from the world. For thousands of years, Jews had been prevented from associating with outsiders, and now outsiders are being invited to church, and they didn't know what to do with that. When both became Christians, it created an apparent paradox.

So they would be wondering about eating meat sacrificed to idols and if that was OK. Paul answers:

> Now about food sacrificed to idols: We know that we all possess knowledge. Knowledge puffs up, but love builds up. The man who thinks he knows something does not yet know as he ought to know. But the man who loves God is known by God.
>
> So then, about eating food sacrificed to idols: We know that an idol is nothing at all in the world and that there is no God but one. (1 Cor. 8:1–4)

Yes, it's OK, Paul says. Idols are nothing at all in the world, and eating that meat is not sinful. You have permission through the blood of Jesus Christ to eat.

A contemporary parallel might be alcohol. Can you drink? Sure. There is nothing in the Bible that condemns having a drink. But before you go out and buy some beer, keep reading:

> But not everyone knows this. Some people are still so accustomed to idols that when they eat such food they think of it as having been sacrificed to an idol, and since their conscience is weak, it is defiled. (1 Cor. 8:7)

Although we have the liberty to eat that meat, or to drink that alcohol, not everyone will understand this. For those who do not share in this knowledge, eating meat sacrificed to idols is sin because they are sinning against their conscience. Thus while it is not innately sinful, it can be sinful to some. So what should those who do not find it sinful do?

> But food does not bring us near to God; we are no worse if we do not eat, and no better if we do.
>
> Be careful, however, that the exercise of your freedom does

> not become a stumbling block to the weak. For if anyone with a weak conscience sees you who have this knowledge eating in an idol's temple, won't he be emboldened to eat what has been sacrificed to idols? So this weak brother, for whom Christ died, is destroyed by your knowledge. When you sin against your brothers in this way and wound their weak conscience, you sin against Christ. Therefore, if what I eat causes my brother to fall into sin, I will never eat meat again, so that I will not cause him to fall. (1 Cor. 8:8–13)

No, it's not sinful to eat or drink what causes some to have doubts. But if the exercise of your freedom causes your brother to stumble, it is sin. I know a church that promotes using vulgar language for fun because they have the freedom to do so. Some of these people exercise their freedom in a way that can be destructive to the faith of those around them. What they are doing may not be sinful in itself, but the way they're doing it is. For in causing their brother to sin, they sin against Christ.

In the end it is not about liberty. It is not about the law. It is about love. We ought to share Paul's attitude:

> I will not do anything that will cause my brother or sister to stumble.
> I know I have the freedom to do this, but I don't want to.
> I don't want to do anything that could hurt another's faith.
> So because I love others more than my own rights, I will lay down my rights.

Can you imagine what a church would look like if we all put that into practice?

You know what Paul asks us to do? To follow Jesus. Jesus "who, being in very nature God, did not consider equality with God something to be grasped, but made himself nothing, taking the very nature of a servant" (Phil. 2:6–7). Jesus laid down His rights as God to come to earth and die on a cross to remove all the obstacles between man and God because He loved us. Shouldn't we, His followers, lay down our rights in order to remove obstacles from the paths of others? Shouldn't we love at least that much?

A selfless community where each person loves others more than themselves is a community that will inevitably be full of life. Selfishness creates zombies. Selflessness, expressed in love, makes us more like Jesus

Chapter Eleven

AWAKENING THE UNDEAD

A common frustration that I have with zombie movies is the stupidity of the characters. A vast majority of the time, the plot of the movie is progressed by main characters making bad decisions. The absence of this plot flaw made the 2010 film *The Crazies*[1] a refreshing change of pace. The main character, David Dutton (played by Timothy Olyphant), is a local sheriff who makes all the right decisions. He pays attention, and because of that he realizes what's going on before it's too late. His response to the zombie problem in his town enables him to survive in situations where the people around him do not. Surviving a Zombie church I imagine isn't much different than surviving in a zombie movie: realizing what's going on and doing something before it's too late is key.

I heard a story about a four-year-old named Billy who had a pet cat. One day while Billy was at school, his cat was run over by a car. Wanting to protect her son from seeing his beloved kitty dead on the road, his mother quickly disposed of the remains. A few days went by before Billy began asking what had happened to his cat. "Billy, the cat died," his mother explained, then went on to comfort him. "It's all right—now he's up in heaven with God." Billy was puzzled by his mother's statement. So he asked, "What in the world would God want with a dead cat?"

Have you ever noticed how kids have this strange ability to make these statements that force us to stop and reevaluate how we think? Dead cats aside, I do want to ask a similar question: What in the world would God want with a dead church?

Wake Up!

In Revelation 2 and 3, we see seven letters to seven different churches in Asia Minor. This portion of the text comes from the mouth of Jesus Himself. In each of these letters Jesus says: *I know. I know your deeds. I know your afflictions.* This is very personal. Jesus says, *I know how you live.* He is not fooled by our façades. He is not deceived by our titles or reputations; Jesus sees our hearts. He knows what we do and why we do it. These two chapters of Revelation really bring the idea of a personal God into focus.

Now for two of those churches in Asia Minor—Smyrna and Philadelphia—Jesus has no complaints, nothing bad to say. For two of the seven churches—Sardis and Laodicea—Jesus has no compliments, nothing good to say. Can you imagine your local church getting a personal letter from Jesus only to find that He has nothing good to say about you? Ouch. Let's take a look at the church of Sardis:

> To the angel of the church in Sardis write:
>
> These are the words of him who holds the seven spirits of God and the seven stars. I know your deeds; you have a reputation of being alive, but you are dead. Wake up! Strengthen what remains and is about to die, for I have not found your deeds complete in the sight of my God. Remember, therefore, what you have received and heard; obey it, and repent. But if you do not wake up, I will come like a thief, and you will not know at what time I will come to you.

> Yet you have a few people in Sardis who have not soiled their clothes. They will walk with me, dressed in white, for they are worthy. He who overcomes will, like them, be dressed in white. I will never blot out his name from the book of life, but will acknowledge his name before my Father and his angels. He who has an ear, let him hear what the Spirit says to the churches. (Rev. 3:1–6)

Sardis was established in 2600 B.C. It was built on a mountain about fifteen hundred feet above the valley floor. The only way you could even approach the city was from a steep path to the south. In 680 B.C. it became the capital of Lydia. It was a wealthy and powerful city with mighty fortress walls and considered impossible to conquer. Yet in 546 B.C. Cyrus the Great of Persia conquered it.[2] But just wait until you hear how.

When the people of Lydia went to war with the Persians, they didn't do very well. After being defeated on a few occasions, Croesus the Lydian general had all his forces withdraw inside the walls of Sardis. Croesus did not think the siege would last long, so he planned to just wait them out in the city. Now this is the really sad part. Here is how Sardis fell. Cyrus noticed that while the people were locked inside, there were no guards along the walls. The soldiers were not at their post. They had fallen asleep. They felt so safe and secure inside their impenetrable walls that the people stopped paying attention to the threat at their door. So, completely unhindered, the Persians climbed up the wall, opened the gates, and sacked the city. That has to be one of the most embarrassing stories of defeat in military history. The unconquerable city falls without killing a single enemy soldier.

A few centuries later, in 214 B.C., Antiochus III, called Antiochus the Great, conquered Sardis because the people inside had fallen asleep. No one was at their guard station and so Antiochus's soldiers climbed the wall, opened the gate, and conquered the city. Two times in their history Sardis had been defeated because they were not prepared. (Conquer me once because I am asleep, shame on you; conquer me twice because I am asleep, shame on me.)

Now look at the point that Jesus drives home in this letter: *wake up!* Jesus connects this letter to the history of the city. Here you are sitting inside your walls feeling so safe and secure. You think you're strong. You think you're alive but you're not. If you don't wake up, you are going to be destroyed. The church in Sardis was following the example of the history of its people. They were asleep. The church was dying and what in the world could God want with a dead church? Do you see how personal this letter is?

God is not getting His list of who will be saved from church rosters.

There's another personal aspect of this letter to the church of Sardis. Sardis was the register of the Persian and Seleucid empires so anyone who was part of the empire had their names on record in Sardis. But if that person committed treason or died, their name was blotted out of the register. Jesus says, *I have a book of life. If you overcome, I will never blot your name out of My register.* God is not getting His list of who will be saved from church rosters.

For those who are Christian in name only, their names will be blotted out of the book of life. They will be denied access to the kingdom of God. It is not enough to look alive if we do not have the life of God in us. The church in Sardis is not noted for any immorality or false teaching. We are not told of any great sin they committed. Their only problem was that they were asleep.

We have a lot in common with the church of Sardis. We have built mighty walls in the fortresses of our church. There is a great army at our gates seeking to destroy us. But this is not nap time. If we want to survive, we need to wake up. We must stay alert. A church that has fallen asleep will eventually be destroyed.

All the evil and depravity of the world is not because evil is overcoming good but because good isn't fighting back. As British statesman Edmund Burke is thought to have said: "All that is necessary for the triumph of evil is that good men do nothing." Light and dark are not equal and opposite forces

Light and dark are not equal and opposite forces in the world.

in the world. Darkness does not overcome light; darkness is just the absence of light.

Darkness can only exist where the light has gone out. As Christians we are the light of the world (Matt. 5:14–16). Our purpose is to shine in the darkness. We cannot shine in the darkness if we are locked away safely in our church walls. We need to show the world what Jesus looks like and to be light in their lives.

In Revelation 2 and 3, each of these letters ends the same: "He who has an ear, let him hear what the Spirit says to the church." In other words, *wake up!* Jesus is calling the church to *be* the church. God isn't interested in what you call yourself; He is interested in who and what you really are. We need to let God into our lives and let Him fill us with so much love that we have no choice but to go into the world and to share it with others.

Radical and Dynamic

Not that long ago I started thinking about my life, and I realized that something was missing. I prayed when I was supposed to pray, I read the Bible and studied it all the time, I quoted it, used it, preached it . . . but still I felt like something was missing. In doing all the things I was supposed to do, I felt drained.

I had developed some bad habits. As my entire day revolved around reading and studying the Word of God, the Bible became my job. I thought that was OK. What's wrong with being a professional Christian? And then I figured it out. In making myself a professional Christian, I had become an amateur child of God. I know some of you know exactly what I mean because you've felt it too. Sometimes we spend all our time and energy going through the religious motions and we forget who we really are. It is easy to pretend to be a Christian, but God knows the truth we sometimes try to hide from ourselves.

The church has given us rules and regulations. Things that, supposedly, you must do to be a Christian. Do all these things so that you will look good, so the church will look good. You know what most of those rules remind me of? The Pharisees. I don't see Jesus playing by any of those rules. Sometimes we make following Jesus so complicated when really it is very simple.

Sometimes we make following Jesus so complicated when really it is very simple.

There is something so radical and so dynamic that it can change your life forever; something so big that you cannot do it on your own; something so significant that I really believe that if you do it, you'll make an impact on this world for the kingdom of God. But to get this something, you have to let go of what you have become. I have gone to church my whole life, and I don't know if I really understood what it meant to follow Jesus until recently.

My closest friend in school was not a Christian. She was close. She *wanted* to believe in God, but she had not seen Him in the church. I had tried on occasion to talk with her about Jesus, but I didn't get very far. One day I had a breakthrough and she agreed to come to an event with me. She arrived and I was so excited. I introduced her around and tried to get some of the other kids to befriend her.

But she wasn't dressed right. A group of girls glared at her the whole time because she was wearing an outfit they considered inappropriate. She felt very uncomfortable, and she never came back. I gave up. For three years we were friends and I didn't say what I should have said. She is not a Christian, she does not know Jesus, and that's partly because I failed to say what I needed to say. I used to think that was OK.

I used to think that when someone rejected Jesus, she fully understood who He was and chose to ignore Him. Over the years that thinking has changed in my mind. I believe that a large number of people who are not Christians are not Christians because they have never recognized the love of Jesus in their lives. It's not because they haven't heard about Him but because they have not seen Him in the lives of His followers. It is not our job to just tell the world about Jesus; it is our job to show the world Jesus.

So if you are bored with the church, if you are looking for something

It is not our job to just tell the world about Jesus; it is our job to show the world Jesus.

with meaning, with power, something that makes a difference in your life, then what you are looking for is simple. You are looking for something that can revolutionize the way we do church; something that changes . . . everything. There is something like that. Some*one*, actually. His name is Jesus and He changes everything. What has been missing for so long in the church is *Jesus*.

I doubt that's what you were expecting. "Church is all about Jesus, so how can He be the cure to zombiism?" you ask. Yes, church is *supposed* to be about Jesus. Churches with *life* are about Jesus. The condition that besets the church today is that so many churches have become about other things entirely. Jesus might be talked about, but He is not the focus of their existence.

In our religious practices we have been so good at going through the motions that we didn't even notice that Jesus left the room. He didn't abandon us. He invited us to follow, but amidst our clanging cymbals we didn't hear Him. Someone once even painted a famous picture of this: Jesus outside knocking on the door of the church, wanting to get back inside! If you are seeking purpose and life, what you are seeking is Jesus.

The Pharisees took the law of God and used it to look good on the outside, but in passionately following Jesus our concern is not just about the appearance but about the reality. As we take steps to follow Jesus in our lives, He begins to work on our hearts. When we slowly allow God to shape and mold our hearts, we become more like Christ. We become filled with His love and passion for this world. Without this inward change, even our best actions are nothing more than a cheap façade. We must let go of our hearts and have a heart like Jesus.

A Bleeding Heart

From Genesis to Malachi, God's love is made known throughout Scripture. He reveals His heart to us that we may know where we stand with Him, and we need to see God's heart if we want to be God's church.

> The Lord appeared to us in the past, saying:
> "I have loved you with an everlasting love;
> I have drawn you with loving-kindness.
> I will build you up again
> and you will be rebuilt, O Virgin Israel."
> (Jer. 31:3–4)

God's love is everlasting. Israel was not the most faithful of nations. Throughout the nation's history, its people turned away from God. Israel exchanged His truth for the lies of the world. Yet God still loves Israel, for His love is everlasting. The same holds true today. Even when the church isn't what it is supposed to be, God still loves the church. He is still willing to save her.

> Praise the Lord, O my soul,
> and forget not all his benefits—
> who forgives all your sins
> and heals all your diseases,
> who redeems your life from the pit
> and crowns you with love and compassion.
> (Ps. 103:2–4)

God is a God who heals. He will forgive the sins that we have committed. He will redeem the life of His people. God still believes in the church, and so long as that remains true, which it will always be, the church is worth defending. She is not beyond saving. God is willing. God is able. Look at what He says in Hosea:

> How can I give you up, Ephraim?
> How can I hand you over, Israel?
> How can I treat you like Admah?
> How can I make you like Zeboiim?
> My heart is changed within me;
> all my compassion is aroused.

> I will not carry out my fierce anger,
> nor will I turn and devastate Ephraim.
> (Hos. 11:8–9)

God's heart bleeds and breaks for the lost. No matter how many times we turn from Him, God is faithful even when we are not. He is ready and willing to offer life to all who will come to Him. His heart is filled with so much love that it cannot be contained.

Loving parents will do just about anything to protect their kids. Can you imagine how hard it would be for a father to knowingly sacrifice his child? Yet that is exactly what God did. He gave the life of His Son so that He could give life to us. His love for us was so great that He was willing to sacrifice His firstborn child. Oh how great a love that must be that God has poured out on us even when we don't deserve it!

For those of you who have been burned by the church, you might think, *Well, the church is so messed up it doesn't deserve to be saved.* And you'd be right. But then again, you don't deserve to be saved either. God loves the church just as God loves you: not because any of us *deserves* it but because God *is* love.

God's love for you is unconditional; it's not dependent on anything. The world, on the other hand, loves you for how you make it feel. I heard of a couple who were happily married for a number of years. One day the wife got in a car accident and had to be taken to the hospital. She survived the accident but was disfigured. In a few weeks, her husband told her he was leaving because he just didn't love her anymore.

God does not need you to be great. He just loves you.

God's love is not based on how attractive you are or how fit or athletic you might be. God's love is not based on your talent, your abilities, or your strengths. It does not matter how poor you are, how many mistakes you have made, how many times you have failed, or how many friends you have. God does not need you to be great. He just loves you. And He will always love you. Nothing you can do will take that away, because the love that God has for you is not based on who you are but on who He is. God's love has no conditions. It has no limits. It just is.

That is the beauty of God's love. You do not have to impress Him. You do not have to entertain Him. He just wants to be with you. He already sent His only Son to die a horrible death so that He might be with you. He loves you that much. Words cannot describe, thoughts cannot express, and songs cannot capture just how great God's love for you really is.

The story of the prodigal son constantly captures my heart (Luke 15:11–32). The son tells his dad, "I wish you were dead," then goes off and wastes all his inheritance. After living the life he thought he wanted for a while, the son realizes that it doesn't satisfy. So he decides to go home and beg his father to allow him to be a servant. While he is still a long way off, his father sees him and comes running. The father *runs*. Distinguished Jewish men did not run; it was degrading. But the father doesn't care. When he sees his son returning home, he runs to him.

This is *our* story. We are the ones who have gone away, but if we would just come to Him . . . if we would just realize that we have wronged Him and just start heading home . . . He will not wait for you to get to the door. He is not preparing a lecture so when you get home He can say, "I told you so." He is not looking to embarrass or humiliate you. If you would just go to Him . . . then *He* would come running to you. He wants you to come home. He wants you to be with Him.

God accepts you as you are; loves you as you are. He calls you to be His child and to be a part of His kingdom. "How great is the love the Father has lavished on us, that we should be called children of God!" (1 John 3:1). So . . . if God doesn't give up on us even though we are imperfect, how can we give up on the church when it is imperfect?

The Key to Life and Love: Jesus

Zombie churches make church about a lot of different things. For some it's about the music. For some it's the classes. For some it is the good feeling of being accepted by others. For some it is power. For others it's tradition.

The church is ever, only, always about Jesus.

There are no shortage of things we can make the church about that have nothing to do with God's true design for His bride. The church is ever, only, always about Jesus. Everything else is just a form of idolatry. Jesus is the center, the focus. He is not just a part of what we do: it's all about Him and for Him.

In order to follow Jesus, we must follow the example that He set for us. Jesus did not live His life off by Himself. The only times when Jesus was really alone was when He went away to reconnect with God. The rest of the time Jesus lived with a radical investment to a radical community. Jesus touched people's lives.

Throughout His ministry, the religious leaders accused Jesus of eating with the wrong people. They asked why He ate with tax collectors and sinners. One of my professors had a great answer: because Jesus doesn't like to eat alone. Jesus lived in relationship with people who did not have the life of God. His purpose was to bring life to the sick and the dying. Jesus is holistically welcoming.

Jesus looked at people whom no one else would see and Jesus saw their needs. He touched people no one else would touch and He healed them. And, most importantly, Jesus loved people whom no one else would love. That is exactly what some of us have missed in the church. We go, thinking we will find a safe place where people will see us and love us, and then when Christians fail to do either, we start to lose hope.

Just because a church is warm and inviting when you show up doesn't mean it's alive. A church can be friendly without being inclusive. It's like going to Disneyland. The workers are very personable, they just aren't personal. When you leave, they don't follow up with you. While they are engaging, they are not really investing. They don't become a part of your life. This is sometimes the way of things in the church. We are glad when people show up. We want them to come to the church, but we are just not really interested in inviting them into our lives.

Yet while the church may miss things, Jesus never does. He sees you,

and He loves you. Jesus didn't invite people to church services. He didn't introduce Himself during the greeting time and then turn His back. Jesus was constantly inviting people into His life: poor people, sick people, sinners, tax collectors, and even Samaritans.

Religion is radically *ex*clusive. Religion says if you want life, you have to do things exactly how we tell you to. Our way is the only way and every other way is wrong. If you are not a part of this specific church, well, you might just burn in hell. In "religious" churches, it's not enough to believe in Jesus and serve Him as your Lord and Savior.

Religion is exclusive and one of the primary things that it excludes is *life*.

Jesus is inclusive. Jesus invites people no one else would even want in order to establish a kingdom where all are welcome no matter their age, gender, denomination, or country. The only requirement for being a part of this kingdom is that you love Jesus enough to follow Him. John tells us what following Jesus looks like:

> Dear friends, let us love one another, for love comes from God. Everyone who loves has been born of God and knows God. Whoever does not love does not know God, because God is love. This is how God showed his love among us: He sent his one and only Son into the world that we might live through him. This is love: not that we loved God, but that he loved us and sent his Son as an atoning sacrifice for our sins. Dear friends, since God so loved us, we also ought to love one another. No one has ever seen God; but if we love one another, God lives in us and his love is made complete in us. (1 John 4:7–12)

Following Jesus means you love like Jesus. When you love like Jesus, you live like Jesus. When we live like Jesus, we start to look like Jesus and the world can see Jesus in us. This is what brings life to the church. We must be willing to lay aside all the complicated things of religion and get back to the simplicity of following Jesus. If we hold on to tradition for the sake of tradition, we miss out on life. If we follow rules expecting them to make us holy, we miss out on life. If we consider ourselves the judges of the world and treat outsiders as dirty sinners, we miss out on life. Life comes from Jesus. It manifests itself in the form of genuine love.

Revived

It is not uncommon for us to treat church as a building that we go to on Sunday mornings, and to build our church identity around the building and the denomination. We come to church, we worship, and we leave because for many of us, church is still a place we go instead of who we are.

We need to let the old church go and become something new.

It is very rare to see churches (much less, denominations) working together on a regular basis—despite the fact that we have the same goal and are serving the same God.

In order for us to revive the church, we need to establish unity within the church—not just within a single church building but among the people: all Christians everywhere. We need to stop being the stagnant church that stows ourselves away in a building and start becoming a community of common-minded people working for the glory of their King by going out into the world and connecting people with Jesus. We need to let the old church go and become something new.

So let us become a new church, a church that is not program-driven but people-driven. Let us become a church that is more concerned for the lost and the hurting than for the average weekly attendance. About a hundred years ago, the flame of life came roaring through the church with a call for restoration, to let go of all the legalistic practices and self-righteous routines and to become "Christian only." The restoration revived the church by reminding it of its purpose.

That is what we need today. We need to wake up every morning and ask ourselves, "How can I be Jesus in someone's life today?" We need to find practical ways every day to show people the love of Jesus. You may not change the world (all at once), but you will change the lives of people around you. In turn they will change the lives of those around them and, before long, life will reign in the church.

Love did it before, and love will do it again.

Chapter Twelve

SEARCHING FOR THE CURE

If one word was all that was allowed to describe the person of God, that word would have to be *love*. This is without a doubt the most defining characteristic of His nature. God without love is like an Oreo cookie without the crème center. God without love is not God. God loves the unlovable. God loves those who don't deserve love. God loves the imperfect, the broken, the lost. God loves: without distinction, without calculation, without procrastination, without condition. God loves.

God loves the church. So much so that in Scripture Jesus refers to the church as His bride. In essence the love between a husband and wife is a physical representation of the love that God has for His church. He loves her so much that He sent His Son to give His life for her.

The first mark of a living church is love. John Piper says: "Genuine love is so contrary to human nature that its presence bears witness to an extraordinary power."[1] When we love each other, our lives become a testimony to the power and the person of God, and when others see it, many will be drawn to it, will be drawn to God.

It's hard to watch people destroy each other. It's hard to watch as they make decisions that you know will cause pain. When we get together we sometimes hurt each other because we all are broken. All are flawed. All are human. It sort of makes you wonder, why even try? What is the point of starting another relationship that will cause pain? Is it worth it? This question may be what keeps us from connecting to the community of God's people. The answer is unquestionably, unreservedly yes. It is worth it. Love is always worth it.

I had a friend who was really struggling at his church. He would get frustrated and upset at the people there because they didn't seem to get what being a Christian was all about. They could be petty and childish. They could be selfish and cruel. "What's the point of being a part of the church if the church is going to behave like this?" he asked. One day he got his answer. A storm hit his life and messed him up pretty good. In his time of need, those same selfish, cruel, petty people rallied together to support and encourage him. They were there for him and helped him in any way they could. Seeing the church in the midst of his storm opened his eyes to a whole new picture of the church. The church is not always perfect but it has purpose. When love takes hold of our hearts and we start living and acting in love, love begins the process of perfecting us.

In 1 Corinthians, Paul devotes almost three chapters to the subject of spiritual gifts—a problem the Corinthians were struggling with. They had put too much emphasis on certain gifts, and Paul is writing to correct their focus. What Paul says is that even if you have the greatest gifts and you know everything—if you have insight into hidden truths, if you can move mountains, even if you can speak in foreign tongues, heal the sick, cast out demons, and raise the dead—if you do all these things but do not have love, these things are meaningless. It's good to desire the greater gifts . . . as long as you understand that the greatest of these gifts is *love*.

To love someone who doesn't deserve it, to forgive the wrong things that were done to you years ago without demanding reparation be made,

Without love service means nothing. Without love faith means nothing.

to love unlovable people is a supernatural gift that comes only from a relationship with God. No matter how significant what you do is, if you do it without love, it means nothing. Without love service means nothing. Without love faith means nothing.

Like the church in Corinth, we can get distracted when it comes to spiritual gifts. There are people who are spiritually immature and ignorant of God's Word, and yet they are interested in gifts. They haven't laid a proper foundation for their life, but they are trying to figure out the nature and expression of spiritual gifts. This is like taking a math class on the dynamics of quantum systems before taking algebra. When you don't build on the basics, then you'll have difficulty accurately understanding complexities. *First,* we need a firm grasp on how to love like Jesus.

When I first started at Cornerstone, a couple came in for a service. I had never seen them before, so I went over and introduced myself. He asked me what the church's stance on speaking in tongues was, and I explained that while we have some people who are for it and others who are against it, we do not publicly practice it in our church services. He got very upset and said he was going to finish his coffee and leave because he wouldn't go to a church that denied the Holy Spirit. Reactions like this are not uncommon when it comes to spiritual gifts because we focus too much on them. We act in unloving ways when we don't agree and thus we show our ignorance of what the Spirit is trying to teach us in 1 Corinthians—that love is far more important than any other gift.

Love *Is* and Love *Does*

First Corinthians 13 has been called the "greatest, strongest, deepest thing Paul ever wrote."[2] Before we can honestly evaluate if we really love or if this is an area we need to work on, we need to know what love is—the internal reality—and what love does—the outward display. Paul shows us both:

> If I speak in the tongues of men and of angels, but have not love, I am only a resounding gong or a clanging cymbal. If I have the gift of prophecy and can fathom all mysteries and all knowledge, and if I have a faith that can move mountains, but have not love, I am nothing. If I give all I possess to the poor and surrender my body to the flames, but have not love, I gain nothing.
>
> Love is patient, love is kind. It does not envy, it does not boast, it is not proud. It is not rude, it is not self-seeking, it is not easily angered, it keeps no record of wrongs. Love does not delight in evil but rejoices with the truth. It always protects, always trusts, always hopes, always perseveres.
>
> Love never fails. But where there are prophecies, they will cease; where there are tongues, they will be stilled; where there is knowledge, it will pass away. For we know in part and we prophesy in part, but when perfection comes, the imperfect disappears. When I was a child, I talked like a child, I thought like a child, I reasoned like a child. When I became a man, I put childish ways behind me. Now we see but a poor reflection as in a mirror; then we shall see face to face. Now I know in part; then I shall know fully, even as I am fully known.
>
> And now these three remain: faith, hope and love. But the greatest of these is love. (1 Cor. 13:1–13)

When we look at a text like this and we see love laid out so clearly in front of us, we should naturally evaluate ourselves to see how we are doing.

First Paul discusses what love *is*. Love is patient and kind; these are the positive characteristics. To lack patience or kindness is to lack love. Then we see what love is not: proud, rude, self-seeking, easily angered. A husband with a short temper who yells at his wife is not loving, no matter how much he professes to love his wife. Love is a verb, an action word. The four letters mean nothing by themselves if they are not supported by actions. Love must be humble, considerate, selfless, and self-controlled. If that is not the nature of your heart, then you have work to do; your love is not fully mature. The

Love doesn't care about what is fair for itself but rejoices when others are blessed and mourns when they suffer.

best portrait of what love is comes from Jesus. Jesus stepped into human history to live as a man so that through Him we could be reconnected to God. Jesus never sinned. He never did anything wrong. Yet Jesus took responsibility for our sin. He paid the price for us so that we could have life. Perhaps this is the best way to understand love: love is responsible. Love will take the blame even when love is not the culprit. Taking responsibility for another person's mistake is a beautiful display of love. Love looks like a cross. It is best seen in a willingness to die for the well-being of another. Most of the time that death will not take the form of physical death but of death to one's self—death to our wants, our desires, our preferences, our ego. Love puts others first.

The whole point is that love isn't about you. It is about valuing others more than yourself. So whether that is resisting the urge to mutter obscenities at the person who cuts you off in traffic or encouraging a co-worker who gets the promotion that you felt you deserved, one thing remains consistently true: love considers others long before it ever thinks about itself. Love doesn't care about what is fair for itself but rejoices when others are blessed and mourns when they suffer. Love doesn't worry about what it gets because it is too busy focusing on what it can give. As soon as the great "I/me/my" gets in the equation, it stops being love. For true love is a radical refusal to think of yourself in any given situation. Love is in no uncertain terms a sacrifice given out of joy.

Then Paul moves to what love *does*—its visible external qualities, which are directly affected by what love is. If you truly love, then these actions will naturally be evident in your life. Again Paul will state these in both positive and negative ways.

With love, people will protect, trust, hope, persevere, rejoice in truth. Without love, people will envy, boast, keep record of wrongs, delight in evil. So when we see ourselves doing the things that love does, we can know that we are loving. When we see ourselves doing the things that love does not do, then we know we are not loving and need to change the way we live.

One of these really gets me: love always perseveres. Love is not a single moment in which we are patient or kind. A lot of my friends have been through bad relationships, and when it was over, they would say, "She was nice when we first met." Or, "He used to be so thoughtful [or romantic, or generous, etc.]." The bottom line is, there wasn't really love there. True love would have continued to do those things. In a romantic love relationship, if you don't "finish the race," then you haven't exercised true love. Love won't quit when trials and hardships come along. Perseverance includes all the other characteristics as well: we will *keep on* being patient, we will *keep on* being selfless. You get the idea.

Love only fails when we fail to love.

This is also true in our relationship with God. If we do not stay true to Him, even under trials and persecution, then we do not really love Him. Love only fails when we fail to love.

I find it amusing when people talk about the loving feeling they have for each other. We often think of love like snuggling up to a fire on a cool winter night; it just fills you with nice toasty feelings all over. People who think like this don't know what love is. Erwin McManus writes in his book *The Barbarian Way* that love is not so much a guarantee of warm feelings and happiness as it is a promise of pain.[3]

The more you love someone, the more you give them permission to hurt you. In case you haven't heard it already, let me be the one to tell you: love is not an emotion. Loving like Jesus is not about having warm fuzzy feelings toward people; it is about living a lifestyle where we impact the world like Jesus did.

Where are you with these characteristics? I want you to read over Paul's passage again and ask yourself which of these characteristics needs improvement. None of us loves as well as we should; every one of us needs to fix at least one of these areas in our lives (and if you're feeling pretty good about your self-evaluation, then you probably need to work on humility). Let this passage be our training manual to loving like Jesus and let us not stop until we have perfected our love.

Now the temptation we face in looking at this is to turn love into a new law:

I need to be patient.

I have to be kind.

I can't be so easily angered.

We see this list and we focus on how to live and we turn it into a law that we follow. Not only does this undermine grace, but it makes our lives more difficult than they need to be. There is a better answer than trying to train yourself to play by the rules: *seek a relationship.*

In a relationship there is some natural adaptation that occurs. When you spend a considerable amount of time with someone, certain aspects of their personality will naturally rub off on you. (I notice this with my wife all the time. I can tell which friends she has hung out with recently because she has picked up on some of their mannerisms.) And the closer you are to that person, the greater this effect will be. Unhealthy relationships will become a negative influence on your life. As Paul paraphrases Proverbs, "Bad company corrupts good character" (1 Cor. 15:33; cf. Prov. 22:24–25). In healthy relationships, however, this is very useful. Instead of trying to turn love into a set of rules that we focus on doing, focus on the One who loves more than anyone else. You don't have to *train* yourself to love, you just have to spend time with the Author of love. The more time you spend with God, the more His character (love) will rub off on you. Then we will become love as He begins to fill us with His love.

The most important commandment is to love God with all that you are. That is the foundation for learning how to love like Jesus. The second most important commandment is to love your neighbor as yourself. The whole Old Testament law is summed up in these two commands. If we want to love like Jesus, this is where it starts: we have to love our neighbor. John writes of love with a strange degree of familiarity:

> If anyone says, "I love God," yet hates his brother, he is a liar. For anyone who does not love his brother, whom he has seen, cannot love God, whom he has not seen. And he has given us this command: Whoever loves God must also love his brother. (1 John 4:20–21)

John and his brother, James, were given the name Boanerges, the Sons of Thunder (Mark 3:17). These guys were passionate, vindictive, and maybe even obsessed with their own fame and glory. They wanted to cast down fire from heaven to destroy a Samaritan village that did not welcome Jesus because He was a Jew. Later John saw an exorcist casting out demons in Jesus' name and demanded that he cease because he was not a disciple. Throughout Jesus' ministry we see John is passionate and proud. But I want you to picture him differently.

Just picture John as he is writing this epistle. He is an old man—the last living apostle of Christ, one of those who was closest to Jesus while He was on earth. He has watched all of his friends be killed for their faith and has been exiled for his own, and the only thing that he has to say is—his passion is—to preach love. Do you see the power of love just in what he is writing? John has been transformed, from an intemperate youth to a man filled with love. Here's his message:

Love!

Love God!

Love your neighbor!

Love your brother!

Love!

The same man who wanted to sit at Jesus' right hand records a gospel (the book of John) where he does not even mention himself by name. John no longer cares if you know who he is. He wants to be known by the thing that is most important to him: the fact that Jesus loved him. John recognized that he was not special because he was a great speaker or because he was a disciple but simply because Christ loved him.

I am reminded of a girl, I'll call her Jenn, who was waiting tables at a

A church without love is not a church of Jesus.

restaurant. One night she had a table pay with a credit card and then they quickly left. When she returned to the table, she saw they had left a $100 tip on a $60 ticket. She couldn't believe it. At the bottom of the ticket was a short note saying that Jesus loved her. She had another table that same night that paid with a $50 gift card and they left $50 cash in an envelope and on the envelope they had written: Jesus loves you. She couldn't believe it.

In one night two different families changed her life. A friend she worked with told her, "Jenn, God is trying to tell you something." She had grown up going to church and went to every service until she was seventeen. Although she had been itching to go back, it was not until she experienced the kindness of these two strangers that she found her way back. She said this was a defining moment in her life: "I have found my way back home." Strangers helped Jenn find her way back to Jesus. That is what we are talking about—showing unreasonable kindness to others so they may see Jesus' love.

When we love others with what we do, we show them Jesus. When the world looks at us, they should see our love both for each other and for them. A church without love is not a church of Jesus. If we get just one thing right, let it be our love. Let us love others with the unconditional love of Jesus.

The story is told about a pastor who had a woman come to him for counseling. In their session she told him that she hated her husband and she wanted a divorce. But she wanted more than that. She wanted to hurt him because she hated him so much. So the pastor gave her this very unorthodox advice. He told her to go home and act as if nothing was wrong. To be the best wife she could be.

He told her to act like she was madly in love with him: make his favorite diner, watch his favorite shows, and love him to the best of her ability to make him need her love. Then after four months when he had become dependent on her, she could leave him, devastated. The woman grinned happily at the devious plan and went home to put it into effect.

Four months went by and the pastor had heard nothing from the woman, so he contacted her, asking when she wanted to divorce her husband. The woman replied: "Divorce him? Why on earth would I do that? I love him!" You see, love is not an emotion, it's an action. God loved us by sending His Son to save us. Jesus loved us by dying on the cross for us. If you say that you love someone but your actions contradict your words, then you are a liar and the love of God is not in you.

> This is how we know what love is: Jesus Christ laid down his life for us. And we ought to lay down our lives for our brothers. If anyone has material possessions and sees his brother in need but has no pity on him, how can the love of God be in him? Dear children, let us not love with words or tongue but with actions and in truth. (1 John 3:16–18)

Love Like Jesus

Jeff was a pastor of a church in an area where homosexuality was prevalent. He had been ministering to a homosexual couple in his community for some time. Both Chris and Steve were HIV positive. He had talked with these men and shared Jesus with them, but they still did not believe. They had not felt the touch of God in their lives, and as homosexuals in the church they had not experienced His love even from His own people. They had felt rejection, ridicule, and shame from the people who are supposed to be known by their love.

One day Jeff was in his office working on a sermon, and his phone rang. It was Steve, one of the men he'd been witnessing to. Steve asked Jeff to come over because his partner, Chris, was really sick. When Jeff arrived at the house, he was immediately overwhelmed by the foul odor of vomit. Chris was lying on the couch too sick to move, vomit on the floor next to him. Jeff went to the bathroom, got a towel, got down on his hands and knees and started cleaning up the floor. Steve came down the stairs and saw what Jeff was doing. Seeing Jeff kneeling down, cleaning vomit off the floor, Steve later said, "It was then I saw what Jesus looks like; He looks like Jeff."

This is what I am talking about—what loving like Jesus looks like. Jesus was all about caring for others and something as basic as cleaning vomit off the floor may be the thing that opens someone's eyes to the love of Jesus. Giving, serving, and sharing the heart of Jesus through how you live is loving like Him.

We are not all evangelists. We will not all preach sermons and teach lessons, but every one of us is responsible for being Jesus in the lives of the people we know. You don't have to be brilliant, gifted, funny, or rich. Jesus' primary way of showing love wasn't through giving people money. It was through seeing a need they had and finding a way to do something about it.

When I think about showing the love of Jesus, I think about Brady. Brady had a long history with the church and had been burned pretty badly by it. We also had an older gentleman at the church who was amazing. Although he had a hard time getting around and his hands would constantly tremble and shake, on Sunday mornings he would walk up to everyone in the church, give them a hug, sometimes with tears in his eyes, and tell them he loved them. And he meant it.

There are lots of things that love can do, but in the end love always does something.

Brady would go over to visit this older gentleman, help clean up the house, drive him places. Brady looked after him as if he were a part of his family.

You know, that's it.

Loving like Jesus is as simple as caring for people. In order to love like Jesus, we all need to find our own person whom we take care of and show love to by being there for them and helping them when they need it.

Jesus didn't live in the four walls of a church. Jesus' love was seen in what He did for people. Our love will be seen in what we do for people. The first step to really looking like Jesus is loving others regardless of how they treat you. The fact that people don't *deserve* the love you show them is what makes it so powerful. Maybe that means bringing in lunch for a co-worker who is having a hard time with finances. Maybe it means sitting down and offering to talk with someone who is clearly upset. Maybe it means you mow the lawn for an elderly neighbor. Love may be forgiving a family member who hurt you. Or maybe it is as simple as intentionally developing a relationship with a non-Christian and slowly beginning to share Jesus with that person. There are lots of things that love can do, but in the end love always does *something*.

Mercy

When I was in college, I had a really good friend whom I spent a lot of time with. He had just gotten dumped by the girl he was dating and he was a wreck. He pulled away for a while, but after a month or so things went back to normal.

Well, we knew some of the same people, and one day I was talking with one of them and I found out that he had engaged in a very inappropriate relationship with a girl he worked with. It had happened almost a year before, during the time he had pulled away.

I felt betrayed by his secret. We had even talked about the dangers of the very thing he had done. So I told him that he needed to come clean and confess.

He did. He talked with the school, and they decided to show him mercy and let him remain as a student.

I got upset. They gave him mercy, but I wanted justice. I wanted him to pay for the mistake he had made.

Then one day I was writing a sermon about forgiveness, and he came to mind. I realized I had no business preaching that sermon with this gross error in my life. In wishing justice on him, I was getting in the way of love. So I called him and left him a long message about how I had made this big mistake and I was sorry I wasn't there for him when he needed me. He, being a bigger man than I, forgave me. What I realized is that in wishing justice on him, I was not loving like Jesus. For the love of God is a merciful love, revealed to us in preventing us from receiving what we deserve:

> You see, at just the right time, when we were still powerless, Christ died for the ungodly. Very rarely will anyone die for a righteous man, though for a good man someone might possibly dare to die. But God demonstrates his own love for us in this: While we were still sinners, Christ died for us. (Rom. 5:6–8)

Love desires mercy not justice. When you love someone, the result is that you do good things for them, you pray for them, and you are concerned for them. Love never wishes pain on anyone. There are people in our lives who mistreat us. People who deliberately cause us pain. Some people are rude, inconsiderate, selfish, overbearing, unkind. There are unlovely people in this world. Hypocrites, liars, gossips, and cheats. People will treat you in unloving ways. The problem with these people is not that they are unlovable but that they are unloved. Those unlovely people need love more than anyone. Some people just require a little more grace than others.

Some years ago, at a comparative religions conference, the wise and the scholarly were in a spirited debate about what is unique about Christianity. Someone suggested that what set Christianity apart from other religions was the concept of incarnation—the idea that God took human form in Jesus. But someone quickly noted that other faiths also believe that God appears in human form. Another suggestion was offered: What about resurrection—the belief that death is not the final word; that the tomb was found empty? No. Other religions have accounts of people returning from the dead too.

Then, as the story is told, C. S. Lewis arrived late, tweed jacket, pipe, arms full of papers. He sat down and took in the conversation, which had by now evolved into a fierce debate. During a lull, he asked someone, "What's the rumpus about?" A colleague explained that the discussion was aiming to find Christianity's unique trait among the world's religions. "Oh, that's easy," answered Lewis. "It's grace."[4]

The group considered this. Christianity uniquely claims that God's love comes free of charge, no strings attached. No other religion makes that claim. Buddhists, for example, follow an eightfold path to enlightenment.

It's not a free ride. Hindus believe in karma, that your actions continually affect the way the world will treat you, that there is nothing that comes to you not set in motion by your actions. Someone else observed that the Jewish code of the law implies that God has requirements for people to be acceptable to Him, and in Islam God is a God of judgment not a God of love. You live to appease Him. At the end of the discussion, everyone conceded Lewis's point. Only Christianity dares to proclaim that God's love is unconditional. We call it grace. Given to us through Jesus' sacrifice on the cross.

> If there is no resurrection of the dead, then not even Christ has been raised. And if Christ has not been raised, our preaching is useless and so is your faith. More than that, we are then found to be false witnesses about God, for we have testified about God that he raised Christ from the dead. But he did not raise him if in fact the dead are not raised. For if the dead are not raised, then Christ has not been raised either. And if Christ has not been raised, your faith is futile; you are still in your sins. Then those also who have fallen asleep in Christ are lost. If only for this life we have hope in Christ, we are to be pitied more than all men.
>
> But Christ has indeed been raised from the dead, the firstfruits of those who have fallen asleep. For since death came through a man, the resurrection of the dead comes also through a man. For as in Adam all die, so in Christ all will be made alive. (1 Cor. 15:13–22)

To deny the resurrection is to destroy any motivation for ethical behavior within the church, let alone the world.

If all Jesus did was go to the cross, then worshipping Him is worthless. There is no life in the death of Jesus alone. If Christ is not raised, your faith means nothing. If Christ is not raised, you are still trapped in slavery to your sins. If Christ is not raised, there is no life after death. If Christ is not raised, then Christians are to be pitied more than all men. Without the resurrection we have no life, no hope, no meaning, no purpose: this life is all there is. To deny the resurrection is to destroy any motivation for ethical behavior within the church, let alone the world.

However, it is perfectly understandable to put one's self in danger, to live selflessly, and to make sacrifices if there is hope of resurrection.

Resurrection

Too many Christians live like we serve a God who is dead. We worship, we pay tribute, and we honor God like He isn't around anymore. It's like we forget that God seeks a real relationship with us and that He has power not only in the past but for our lives now too. Jesus isn't just some name of a guy who died a long time ago for the good of others: Jesus is the living God. That is what is so great about our faith. We are not worshipping stones and statues but an almighty God who conquered the grave. Since Christ rose from the dead, we have life through Him. Sin and death entered the world through Adam; Jesus is the antidote to the sin problem that Adam created. Adam brought death to all of his children; Jesus brought life to all His people. Jesus is alive and so through Him we may also have life.

Jesus restores that which had been defiled by sin. Through Jesus we ourselves may obtain a resurrection from the dead where we will dwell with Him in paradise forever. Jesus' resurrection means life for all who follow after Him.

Thanks to the grace given to us in Christ Jesus we are alive not just right now, but we have eternal life through the resurrection of our Lord. The question we must ask then is, do we live like the dead who do not have the resurrection? Or do we live like the One who died to give us life?

Let's assume that we want to live like Jesus: where do we go from here? We understand that our goal as the church is to become passionate followers of Jesus. We have learned that it's necessary to love God with all our heart, soul, mind, and strength. We have learned about loving our neighbor as ourselves. How do we go from being a church that *talks* about loving like Jesus to being a church that actually does it?

Love can start with the unbelievably simple. Just write someone an encouraging note. Telling him that you are praying for him. Then tell him *what* you are praying for him (and pray for him, of course). Paul does this in his letters, so it's a biblical practice.

The highlights of my ministry are when I find a card from someone just telling me they appreciate me. People can't hear that enough. I still have every single one, and when I am feeling down I go through and look at those cards. They remind me I may sometimes fail but I am not a failure.

So that could be your first step: just write an encouraging note to all the people in your life, telling them what you appreciate about them and what they mean to you. If note-writing isn't your thing, you can call them, send a text, or talk to them in person, but be intentional about what you say. Each one will probably take ten minutes or less, but I guarantee the investment will make a huge difference in people's lives.

From that simple first step, other steps will follow. Over and over in Jesus' ministry, we see Him having meals with people. Jesus ate with people no one else would eat with. This is a great way to affirm someone's value.

You will be amazed at the opportunities you have to show the love of Jesus. From rejoicing with those who rejoice to mourning with those who mourn and everything in between. Do not be the foolish man who hears the words of God and does not put them into practice. Go. Show the love of Jesus. Spend time with people, encourage them, have a meal together. Go be Jesus to someone. Go demonstrate what a relationship with God looks like by loving someone the way that God loves us: unconditionally and unendingly. Go!

Sometimes we want Jesus to be MapQuest.

Sometimes we want Jesus to be MapQuest. We want directions every step of the way. We want to know where to turn and how long we will be on each road. We want the whole trip mapped out before we will set out on the journey.

But Jesus is not MapQuest. As long as we keep Him in our sights, we'll know we're heading in the right direction. When we do lose sight of Him, we need to immediately search until we find Him again. A Zombie church, when it loses sight of Jesus, tries to pretend it knows where it's going without Him. And then it doesn't take long for them to get totally lost.

Each one of us, whether we are church leaders or not even sure if we are interested in the church at all, must decide if we will follow Jesus. It's a life or death choice that each one of us will make.

Bringing It Home

Zombie churches can do a lot of damage in the world and can make Christians look bad. The church is not perfect. There is no denying that. Sometimes the church has so many problems that it's tempting to just give up and walk away. It's easy to get disillusioned by the church when it makes mistakes. It's easy to look at the church and just see all the things that go wrong. Yet we must not forget to recognize all the things that go right. Even the most stagnant churches can bring people to a relationship with God, and isn't that what it's all about? As Christians we must be concerned for the global mission of God to bring all lost people to salvation. This is a task too big for us. It is a task for a community that partners with God to change the world. The church may seem broken, but it's not beyond repair. As individuals we are not always in the right place in our relationship with God; we sometimes drift off course. Since we *are* the church, this is what causes churches to turn into Zombie churches. An entire church can drift off course when its people move apart from God. But instead of abandoning the church, we each need to stop and catch our bearings again.

There is only one Jesus and He should always be the focal point, the centerpiece, the gravitational center of life, the foundation of the church.

The church has focused its attention on a lot of things. It has jumped from rules to doctrines to causes and each time has come up short of the dynamic life-changing entity it was created to be. The biggest problem in the church is that we focus on lots of things that are not Jesus. There is only one Jesus and He should always be the focal point, the centerpiece, the gravitational center of life, the foundation of the church—which is good news for churches struggling with lifelessness, because getting back to life is as simple as making the focus of your life and everything you do *Jesus.*

The church will make mistakes. The church will miss the point. The church will hurt people. The church will fail. So long as people are a part of it, the church will have her share of problems. But thanks to God there is hope. For in the church there is a purpose. In the church there is healing. In the church there is love. In the church there is hope. In the church there is life and that life is the Son of God. The purpose of the church is not to be perfect but to share the love of God with as many people as possible.

Jesus came into this world with one great purpose: to show us the love of God. He did a lot of things in His time on earth, but none of them were so important as this: Jesus showed us how to love. When we were still sinners, living in rebellion against God, when soldiers beat Him, flogged Him, and nailed Him to a tree for our sins, Jesus never stopped loving us. His final message on our behalf, spoken in front of the very people who had laughed and mocked Him as they tortured Him was, "Father, forgiven them." Love doesn't just give us hope: the love of God gives us life. God's love unites us. It should inspire us. Most of all it should transform us. Being all about Jesus means loving like Jesus.

When we love like Jesus, we fulfill the law. This love must be an unconditional, unlimited, genuine kind of love that we can access only through a direct relationship with the almighty God. When we love like Jesus, we show His love to the world. When we love like Jesus, we heal the church. When we love like Jesus, we become disciples. Loving like Jesus is what makes us live like Jesus. Living like Jesus makes us look like Jesus. When a church of people look like Jesus, then the life that will flow out of them will never be contained by the walls of a building. There is hope for the church that learns to love. That hope, that remedy is in your hands. You can be the instrument of change in the church if you will just step up and love others with the unconditional love of God. For those of you who are unhappy with the failures of the church, my challenge to you is to step up and to do something about it. As John says in his first letter:

> And so we know and rely on the love God has for us.
> God is love. Whoever lives in love lives in God, and God in him. (1 John 4:16)

The key to love is removing yourself from the center of the universe. Once you have done that, removing yourself from the throne of your heart should be relatively easy. The selfish make everything about themselves. The servants make nothing about themselves. Loving like Jesus means living as if you are not a factor in the equation. You do what Jesus commands you to do, you help others, care for those in need, and put people, other people, in front of yourself. You then become an empty vessel. Once you have all the old self out, God can begin to fill you with His love and use you as His instrument of change in the world.

We are not responsible for others. We are responsible for ourselves. So don't worry about what everyone else is doing: get your part right. My final appeal to you is this: *love.* Love God. Love people. Love the church. Love your enemies. Love annoying people. Love lost people. Love hurting people. Love rude people. Love that guy at work who invades your personal space. Just love. If you are going to get one thing right in this life, make it love. Love until you feel like you have nothing left to give, then love some more. Love with the relentless and unwavering love of God. Love when you don't feel like it. Love when it isn't easy. Love when it doesn't make sense. Never stop loving. Love transforms everything. When we fail to live like Jesus, it's because we are failing to live in love. When the church fails to look like His bride, it's because God's people are failing to love. You want to see the church become what it was meant to be? You want to see this world look more like the kingdom of God? You want to see people's lives transformed? Then love. Love is the purest, rawest, most dynamic force in this world. When we love we are starting to look like Jesus and we are following the example that He set for us.

How do you love? You treat everyone like they matter to God. You stop thinking about yourself and you focus all that leftover energy on thinking of others. Put God first, others second, and don't even bother thinking of yourself at all. True life comes from love. It is the ultimate cure to zombiism.

This is my prayer for us:

> Father, give us Your heart and take away our own. Give us Your love that we may love like You. Let us see the world through Your eyes that we may treat people in a way that pleases You. God, let Your love flow through us. Turn us into vessels that pour out Your love without ceasing. Do not let appearances or our own shortcomings get in the way of Your mission for the lost. Let us always protect, always trust, always hope, and always persevere. God, You never fail. With every breath we take, God, let us breathe in Your Spirit and breathe out ourselves. May we be a people who live out Your love in all that we do.

May the blessings of God be upon you, may you know the fullness of His love and mercy, and may you walk with Him all the days of your life.

NOTES

Preface

1. George Barna, "The Crisis of Confidence in the Church" August 3, 2010, http://www.georgebarna.com/2010/08/the-crisis-of-confidence-in-the-church/; George Barna, *Revolution* (Wheaton: Tyndale, 2005); Brian Sanders, *Life After Church: God's Call to Disillusioned Christians* (Downers Grove, IL: InterVarsity Press, 2007); Wayne Jacobsen and Dave Coleman, *So You Don't Want to Go to Church Anymore: An Unexpected Journey* (Los Angeles: Windblown Media, 2006).
2. Barna, *Revolution*, 36.
3. Brennan Manning quote found in DC Talk's *Jesus Freak* song, "What if I Stumble" (ForeFront Records, 1995).
4. I've been to churches in other countries, but I don't have enough understanding of their culture or background to address the issues they may be facing. So when I refer to the church or the American church, I am referring specifically to the general condition of the church in North America. These trends may exist elsewhere in the world, but I'm not qualified to speak on them.

Chapter 1: Warning Signs

1. Bernard Diederich and Claudia Wallis, "Zombies: Do They Exist?" *Time*, October 17, 1983, http://www.time.com/time/magazine/article/0,9171,952208,00.html; Patrick D. Hahn, "Dead Man Walking: Wade Davis and the Secret of the Zombie Poison," Biology Online, September 4, 2007, http://www.biology-online.org/articles/dead_man_walking.html. Also, see Tracy V. Wilson, "How Zombies Work," HowStuffWorks, http://www.howstuffworks.com/science-vs-myth/strange-creatures/zombie.htm.
2. Dictionary.com, *Dictionary.com Unabridged*. Random House, Inc., s.v., "zombie," http://dictionary.reference.com/browse/zombie (accessed January 12, 2011). The origin of the word *zombie* is interesting: "1871, of West African origin (cf. Kikongo *zumbi* 'fetish;' Kimbundu *nzambi* 'god'), originally the name of a snake god, later with meaning 'reanimated corpse' in voodoo cult. But perhaps also from Louisiana creole word meaning 'phantom, ghost,' from Spanish *sombra* 'shade, ghost.' Sense 'slow-witted person' is recorded from 1936." Online Etymology Dictionary, comp. Douglas Harper, s.v., "zombie," http://www.etymonline.com/index.php?term=zombie (accessed March 17, 2011). In a cultural context, the term can be defined as follows: "According to Haitian belief, a zombie is an individual who has been 'killed' and then raised from the dead by malevolent voodoo priests known as 'bocors.'" Diederich and Wallis, "Zombies: Do They Exist?"
3. My thoughts here have been influenced by John MacArthur. See his sermon "The Church in Prophetic Perspective: The Dead Church," available at http://www.biblebb.com/files/MAC/sg1442.htm.

Chapter 2: Infected

1. *28 Days Later*, DVD, directed by Danny Boyle (Los Angeles: 20th Century Fox, 2003). Film released in 2002.
2. John Polhill, *The New American Commentary: Acts*, vol. 26 (Nashville: Broadman & Holman, 2001), 273.
3. H. B. Mattingly, "The Origin of the Name Christian," *Journal of Theological Studies* 9 (1958): 26–37, http://jts.oxfordjournals.org/.

4. Erwin Raphael McManus, *The Barbarian Way: Unleash the Untamed Faith Within* (Nashville: Thomas Nelson, 2005), 44–45.
5. Elisabeth Elliot, *Through Gates of Splendor: The Event That Shocked the World, Changed a People, and Inspired a Nation* (Peabody, MA: Hendrickson, 2010). Originally published under main title only (New York: Harper, 1957).
6. *Philistine* comes into English through several languages, lastly "from Hebrew *P'lishtim*, 'people of *P'lesheth*' ('Philistia') . . . the word probably is the people's name for itself." *Palestine* comes "from Latin *Palestina* (name of a Roman province), from Greek *Palaistine* (Herodotus), from Hebrew *Pelesheth* 'Philistia, land of the Philistines.' Revived as an official political territorial name 1920 with the British mandate." Online Etymology Dictonary, s.v., "Philistine," http://www.etymonline.com/index.php?term=Philistine; "Palestine," http://www.etymonline.com/index.php?term=Palestine (accessed March 18, 2011).
7. I don't mean to conform in the Romans 8:29 sense of God causing Christians to become more and more like Jesus in their character and conduct—that's a good thing. But conforming in other ways is usually a bad thing when used elsewhere in Scripture. God is not looking for mindless subjugation but for radical transformation.
8. Mark and Patti Virkler, *How to Hear God's Voice* (Shippensburg, PA: Destiny Image Publishers, 2005), 24.
9. Regardless of whether or not they are inclined to connect these verses to the Lord's Supper or the sacrament of the Eucharist, Bible commentators seem to agree that if there is significance to the difference in the shift of verbs more than just a preference of terms, the shift is one of intensity from the usual verb ("eats") used of human eating to a more graphic and vivid word ("gnaw" or "chew") used at the time of how animals eat. Michal E. Hunt, "The Gospel according to John," AgapeBibleStudy.com, 1998, John 6:53–58, http://www.agapebiblestudy.com/John_Gospel/Chapter%206.htm; New American Bible (NAB), John 6:54, textual note 19, http://www.usccb.org/nab/bible/john/john6.htm#foot19; and New English Bible (NET Bible), John 6:54, textual note 85, http://net.bible.org/#!bible/John+6:54.

Chapter 3: The Transformation Process

1. See chapter 2, note 1.
2. I don't mean to imply that laziness is the only infection in Zombie churches. There are many infections that can kill a church. But the sin of idleness is often overlooked, and so I flesh it out by way of illustration.
3. N. T. Wright, *Simply Christian: Why Christianity Makes Sense* (New York: HarperCollins, HarperSanFrancisco 2006), 203–4.
4. T. S. Eliot, *Murder in the Cathedral* (New York: Harcourt, Brace and Company, 1935), pt. 1.

Chapter 4: The Symptoms

1. *Dawn of the Dead,* DVD, directed by Zack Snyder (Burbank, CA: Starz Media/Anchor Bay, 2004). Film released in 2004. Original film directed by George A. Romero released in 1978.
2. John MacArthur, *Twelve Ordinary Men: How the Master Shaped His Disciples for Greatness, and What He Wants to Do with You* (Nashville: Thomas Nelson, W Publishing Group, 2002).
3. Barna Group, "New Marriage and Divorce Statistics Released," March 31, 2008, http://www.barna.org/barna-update/article/15-familykids/42-new-marriage-and-divorce-statistics-released.
4. Barna Group, "New Study Shows Trends in Tithing and Donating," April 14, 2008, http://www.barna.org/barna-update/article/18-congregations/41-new-study-shows-trends-in-tithing-and-donating.
5. Matt Proctor, "To Do List: Find a Church" (chapel sermon delivered at Ozark Christian College, Joplin, Missouri, January 21, 2010).
6. In Acts 2:42, Luke tells us, "They devoted themselves to the apostles' teaching and to the fellowship, to the breaking of bread and to prayer." Many commentators have attempted to explore the richness of what the early believers enjoyed together. A note on Acts 2:42 in the *ESV Study Bible* explains these activities as follows: "The early church was devoted to the *apostles' teaching,* which would have included Jesus' earthly teaching plus what he taught the apostles in his 40 days of resurrection appearances. *Fellowship* (Gk. *koinōnia,* 'participation, sharing') included the sharing of material

goods (v. 44), the *breaking of bread* (vv. 42, 46), which likely covers both the Lord's Supper and a larger fellowship meal, and *prayers* in house meetings and likely also in the temple (vv. 42, 46)." *ESV Study Bible: English Standard Version* (Wheaton: Crossway, 2007), notes for Acts by John Polhill, http://www.esvonline.org/.

7. *New Testament Greek-English Dictionary: Pi–Rho*, ed. Ralph W. Harris and Stanley M. Horton, Complete Biblical Library, vol. 15 (Springfield, MO: World Library Press, 1991), 335.
8. H. Richard Niebuhr, *The Kingdom of God in America* (Chicago: Willet, Clark, 1937; repr., Middletown, CT: Wesleyan University Press, 1988), 193.
9. Biblica, "How many different languages has the Bible been translated into? Statistical Summary provided by UBS World Report, March 2002," Bible FAQs, http://www.biblica.com/bibles/about/19.php. Also, see Wycliffe Bible Translators, "The worldwide status of Bible translation (2010)," Resources, http://www.wycliffe.org/About/Statistics.aspx and Wycliffe's "The Last Languages Campaign," http://www.lastlanguagescampaign.org/LLC.aspx.
10. Peter Berger, "Counting Christians in China," *The American Interest* blog, August 17, 2010, http://blogs.the-american-interest.com/berger/2010/08/17/counting-christians-in-china/.

Chapter 5: The Undead Heart

1. *Undead Alive: A Zombedy*, DVD, directed by Glasgow Phillips (Hollywood: Image Entertainment, 2007). Film released in 2007.
2. Paul F. Lazarsfeld and Robert K. Merton, "Mass Communication, Popular Taste and Organized Social Action," in Lyman Bryson, ed., *The Communication of Ideas: A Series of Addresses* (New York: Institute for Religious and Social Studies; Harper & Bros., 1948). Reprinted in Paul Marris and Sue Thornham, eds., *Media Studies: A Reader*, 2nd ed. (New York: New York University Press, 2000), 22–23, http://www.journalism.wisc.edu/~gdowney/courses/j201/pdf/readings/Lazarsfeld%20P%20et%20al%201948.pdf. First published in *The Communication of Ideas*, which was based principally on lectures delivered between November 1946 and February 1947 at the Institute for Religious and Social Studies.

Chapter 6: Lost Soul

1. *Day of the Dead*, DVD, directed by Steve Miner (Los Angeles: First Look Pictures; Millennium Films, 2008). Film released in 2008. Original film directed by George A. Romero released in 1985.
2. Jacob Neusner and William Scott Green. *Dictionary of Judaism in the Biblical Period: 450 B.C.E. to 600 C.E.* (New York: Macmillan Library Reference, 1996; Peabody, MA: Hendrickson, 1996), 599.
3. William Mounce, *Mounce's Complete Expository Dictionary of Old and New Testament Words* (Grand Rapids: Zondervan, 2006), s.v., "know, *yāda'*," 381.
4. Ralph Martin, Peter H. Davids, eds., *Dictionary of the Later New Testament and Its Development* (Downers Grove, IL: InterVarsity Press, 1997), 638–40.

Chapter 7: The Rotten Mind

1. *The Signal*, DVD, directed by David Bruckner, Dan Bush, and Jacob Gentry (New York: Magnolia, 2008). Film released in 2007.
2. Likewise Jesus prayed for His disciples and for us, "My prayer is not for them alone. I pray also for those who will believe in me through their message" (John 17:20).
3. As great a blessing as technology is in so many ways, social networking has set us back in our understanding of the levels and progression of friendship in many ways. We no longer have to spend time getting to know someone. If we want to share in their lives, we just log on to Twitter or Facebook, check their status, and boom—instant imitation intimacy. God is a bit old-fashioned. He doesn't post His intimate truths on His Facebook page. If you really want to get to know Him, there is only one way to do it: spend time with Him.

Chapter 8: Zombie Strength

1. *We Were Soldiers*, DVD, directed by Randall Wallace (Hollywood: Paramount Pictures, 2002). Film released in 2002.
2. Donald S. Whitney, *Spiritual Disciplines for the Christian Life* (Colorado Springs: NavPress, 1991), 102.
3. In addition to others, the Discovery Institute's Center for Science and Culture (http://www.discovery.org/csc/) is perhaps the best known advocate

of intelligent design creationism. Wikipedia gives a helpful overview of the intelligent design movement with many primary source links: Wikipedia contributors, "Intelligent design," *Wikipedia, The Free Encyclopedia*, http://en.wikipedia.org/wiki/Intelligent_design (accessed April 7, 2010).

4. Rich Deem, "Evidence for the Fine Tuning of the Universe," Evidence for God from Science (GodAndScience.org), http://www.godandscience.org/apologetics/designun.html (last modified June 8, 2006).
5. Jeff Zweerink and Hugh Ross, appendix B, "Where Is the Cosmic Density Fine-Tuning?" in Hugh Ross, *Why the Universe Is the Way It Is* (Grand Rapids; Baker, 2008), 209–11.
6. Rich Deem, "Extreme Fine Tuning—Dark Energy or the Cosmological Constant," Evidence for God from Science (GodAndScience.org), http://www.godandscience.org/apologetics/cosmoconstant.html#n06 (last modified May 16, 2006). For the traditional explanation, see Jason Lisle, "Does the Big Bang Fit with the Bible?" AnswesInGenesis.org, posted April 15, 2010, http://www.answersingenesis.org/articles/nab2/does-big-bang-fit-with-bible#fnMark_1_2_1, in Ken Ham, ed., *The New Answers Book 2: Over 30 Questions on Creation/Evolution and the Bible* (Green Forest, AR: Master Books, 2008).
7. Deem, "Evidence for the Fine Tuning of the Universe"; Zweerink and Ross, appendix B, "Where Is the Cosmic Density Fine-Tuning?" in Ross, *Why the Universe Is the Way It Is*, 210.
8. North America, World-Atlas.us, http://www.world-atlas.us/north-america.htm (accessed March 26, 2011).
9. Hugh Ross, *The Creator and the Cosmos: How the Greatest Scientific Discoveries of the Century Reveal God* (Colorado Springs: NavPress, 1993), 150.
10. Dennis Edwards, fish and wild life biologist and entomologist, personal communication with author, Janurary 25, 2010.

Chapter 9: The Disease Spreads

1. *I Am Legend*, DVD, directed by Francis Lawrence (Burbank, CA: Warner Home Video, 2008). Film released in 2007.
2. United Nations Development Programme, "The World's Priorities? (Annual Expenditure)" in "The State of Human Development," in *Human Development*

Report 1998 (New York: Oxford University Press, 1998), figure 1.12, http://hdr.undp.org/en/media/hdr_1998_en_chap1.pdf. Figures for basic education for all and basic health and nutrition are estimated additional annual costs to achieve universal access to basic social services in all developing countries.

3. Anup Shah, "Causes of Hunger Are Related to Poverty," Globalissues.org, February 21, 2001, http://www.globalissues.org/article/7/causes-of-hunger-are-related-to-poverty (last modified October 3, 2010).
4. Eric Holt-Giménez and Loren Peabody, "From Food Rebellions to Food Sovereignty: Urgent Call to Fix a Broken Food System," *Food First Backgrounder* 14, no. 1 (Spring 2008): 1, http://www.foodfirst.org/en/node/2199. The article is also available under a different title, "The World Food Crisis: What's Behind It and What We Can Do About It," at http://www.cipamericas.org/archives/1547. For additional, up-to-date information, see Food First Institute for Food and Development Policy at www.foodfirst.org.
5. "Chronic Hunger and Obesity Epidemic; Eroding Global Progress," *Worldwatch Institute*, March 4, 2000, http://www.worldwatch.org/, quoted in Anup Shah, "Obesity," Globalissues.org, September 7, 2001, http://www.globalissues.org/article/558/obesity (last modified November 21, 2010).
6. Colleen Cappon and Karlie Pouliot, "New Jeresy Woman Wants to Weigh 1,000 Pounds," FoxNews.com, March 16, 2010, http://www.foxnews.com/health/2010/03/16/new-jersey-woman-wants-weigh-pounds/.

Chapter 10: Zombie Community

1. *Zombieland* DVD, directed by Ruben Fleischer (Culver City, CA: Sony Pictures, 2010). Film released in 2009.
2. I am indebted for the picture of the church as God's theater to Matt Proctor, from his sermon "To Do List: Find a Church" at Ozark Christian College for a chapel service on January 21, 2010.
3. Jacob Neusner, "Pharisaic Law in New Testament Times," *Union Seminary Quarterly Review* 26 (Summer 1971): 337.

Chapter 11: Awakening the Undead

1. *The Crazies*, DVD, directed by Breck Eisner (Beverly Hills: Overture Films/ Anchor Bay Entertainment, 2010). Film released in 2010. Original film directed by George A. Romero released in 1973.
2. Robert Mounce, *The Book of Revelation*, rev. ed., New International Commentary on the New Testament (Grand Rapids: Eerdmans, 1998), 92.

Chapter 12: Searching for the Cure

1. John Piper, *Desiring God: Meditations of a Christian Hedonist*, rev. and exp. ed. (1986; Colorado Springs: Multnomah, 2011), 140.
2. Adolf Harnack, *The Expansion of Christianity in the First Three Centuries*, vol. 1, trans. and ed. James Moffatt (London: Williams & Norgate; New York: G. P. Putnam's Sons, 1904), 183.
3. Erwin Raphael McManus, *The Barbarian Way: Unleash the Untamed Faith Within* (Nashville: Thomas Nelson, 2005), 116.
4. This anecdote comes from "a speech on Lewis given at Calvin College by Lewis scholar Peter Kreeft," quoted in Scott Hoezee, *The Riddle of Grace: Applying Grace to the Christian Life* (Grand Rapids: Eerdmans, 1996), 42.

ABOUT THE AUTHOR

Tyler Edwards is the lead minister of Cornerstone Christian Church in Joplin, Missouri. He graduated from Ozark Christian College in 2006 with dual degrees in Biblical Literature and Christian Ministries, and in 2007 married Erica, a journalism and broadcasting instructor at Pitt State University.

A speaker for retreats and men's groups, Tyler taught a class on the life of Christ to local pastors in Mbale, Uganda. He works with Rapha House, a nonprofit organization that fights child slavery and works to help victims of sexual exploitation get the healing and help they need to live a free life. He was also on the board of directors for a video company that sought to create a global awareness of sex trafficking issues.

Tyler's hope is to see the church regain an exclusively Christ-centered focus and learn to rise above its differences for the sake of the progression of the kingdom of God.